TEACHER'S GUIDE
Every Student Learns

Science

PEARSON

Scott
Foresman

Editorial Offices: Glenview, Illinois • Parsippany, New Jersey • New York, New York
Sales Offices: Needham, Massachusetts • Duluth, Georgia • Glenview, Illinois
Coppell, Texas • Ontario, California • Mesa, Arizona

www.sfsuccessnet.com

Series Authors

Dr. Timothy Cooney
Professor of Earth Science and Science Education
University of Northern Iowa (UNI)
Cedar Falls, Iowa

Dr. James Flood
Distinguished Professor of Literacy and Language
School of Teacher Education
San Diego State University
San Diego, California

Barbara Foots
Science Education Consultant
Houston, Texas

Dr. M. Jenice Goldston
Associate Professor of Science Education
Department of Elementary Education Programs
University of Alabama
Tuscaloosa, Alabama

Dr. Shirley Gholston Key
Associate Professor of Science Education
Instruction and Curriculum Leadership Department
College of Education
University of Memphis
Memphis, Tennessee

Dr. Diane Lapp
Distinguished Professor of Reading and Language Arts in Teacher Education
San Diego State University
San Diego, California

Sheryl Alicia Mercier, Ma.Ed.
Classroom Teacher
Dunlap Elementary School
Dunlap, California

Dr. Karen Ostlund
Director
UTeach | Dell Center for New Teacher Success
The University of Texas at Austin
Austin, Texas

Dr. Nancy Romance
Professor of Science Education & Principal Investigator
NSF/IERI Science IDEAS Project
Charles E. Schmidt College of Science
Florida Atlantic University
Boca Raton, Florida

Dr. William Tate
Chair and Professor of Education and Applied Statistics
Department of Education
Washington University
St Louis, Missouri

Dr. Kathryn C. Thornton
Professor
School of Engineering and Applied Science
University of Virginia
Charlottesville, Virginia

Dr. Leon Ukens
Professor or Science Education
Department of Physics, Astronomy, and Geosciences
Towson University
Towson, Maryland

Steve Weinberg
Consultant
Connecticut Center for Advanced Technology
East Hartford, Connecticut

Dr. Jim Cummins
Professor
Modern Language Center & Curriculum Department
Ontario Institute for Studies in Education
Toronto, Canada

Consulting Author

Dr. Michael P. Klentschy
Superintendent
El Centro Elementary School District
El Centro, California

ISBN: 0-328-14569-6

© Pearson Education, Inc. **3**

Chapter 1 • Plants and How They Grow

Chapter 2 • How Animals Live

Chapter 3 • Where Plants and Animals Live

Chapter 4 • Plants and Animals Living Together

Chapter 5 • Water

Unit C
Physical Science

Unit D
Space and Technology

Overview

Every Student Learns Teacher's Guide is a lesson-by-lesson companion to Scott Foresman *Science*. It has been designed to provide manageable support for teachers and their students who are challenged by language issues in science, no matter what the first language may be.

Every Student Learns Teacher's Guide is built upon the three pillars of English language learning as identified by Dr. Jim Cummins of the University of Toronto.

- Activate Prior Knowledge/Build Background
- Access Content
- Extend Language

Read more about how to use the three pillars to support ESL students in learning the language of science on the following pages.

For every chapter, the **Picture It!** page is a blackline master to use with the How to Read Science page in the Student Edition. Help students use these masters to practice using target reading skills as they read. Each master provides guided practice using a picture or graphic organizer with text. Teaching notes and answers can be found on the page that follows it (Lesson 1 of the chapter).

For every lesson in each chapter, teaching strategies are provided using the three pillars, with scripted direct instruction highlighted in bold type.

- **Activate Prior Knowledge/Build Background** Suggestions are provided to help you relate science concepts and vocabulary to students' experiences using strategies such as brainstorming, discussion, and demonstrations with concrete examples or visual aids (Picture/Text Walk).

- **Access Content** Discussion suggestions are provided in **Picture/Text Walk** to help students use context and picture clues, referring to pictures in the Student Edition.

- **Extend Language** A variety of strategies are provided to help students develop language skills and proficiency in academic language.

You may choose to use any or all of these suggestions and strategies as needed. **Every Student Learns Teacher's Guide** is a flexible tool that will work in a wide range of classrooms. Use these pages in conjunction with the ESL support notes throughout your Teacher's Edition to provide complete support for your second language learners.

Supporting ESL Students in Learning the Language of Science

Dr. Jim Cummins, Professor
Modern Language Center & Curriculum Department
Ontario Institute for Studies in Education
The University of Toronto
Toronto, Canada

Because language is infused into all aspects of the teaching of science, students whose knowledge of English is limited are likely to have difficulty accessing scientific concepts and expressing their understanding of these concepts in oral and written language. Therefore, teachers are faced with the challenge of modifying their instruction in ways that will assist ESL students.

Effective academic language instruction for ESL students across the curriculum is built on three fundamental pillars:

1. Activate Prior Knowledge/Build Background Knowledge
2. Access Content
3. Extend Language

In developing scientific knowledge through language, and language abilities through science, we can apply these three instructional principles in powerful ways.

1. Activate Prior Knowledge/Build Background Knowledge

Prior knowledge is the foundation of learning. When students read a scientific text, they construct meaning by bringing their prior knowledge of language, science, and of the world in general to the text. Students may not explicitly realize what they know about a particular topic or issue. Activating their prior knowledge brings it to consciousness and facilitates learning.

Activating prior knowledge and building background knowledge are important for all students, but particularly for ESL students who may be struggling with unfamiliar vocabulary and grammatical structures in addition to complex new concepts. Building this context permits students to understand more complex language and to pursue more cognitively demanding activities. It lessens the cognitive load of the text and frees up brain power.

Activation of prior knowledge enables teachers to validate ESL students' background experiences and affirm their cultural knowledge. Inviting students to contribute what they already know to the class discussion communicates to students that the cultural and linguistic knowledge they are bringing into the classroom is valuable.

Strategies for activating prior knowledge and building background knowledge.

A variety of strategies to activate students' prior knowledge are embedded in Scott Foresman *Science.*

- **Brainstorming/discussion** This type of language interaction can happen in the context of a whole class, in small groups, or in pairs; for example, students can interview a partner to find out what each one knows about a particular topic. Discussion can also be highly effective in making abstract concepts more concrete and comprehensible.
- **Use of graphic organizers** These can be used to capture the results of brainstorming and discussion. K-W-L- charts, word webs, and many other graphic organizers enable students to record and organize their information.
- **Visuals in texts** Photographs, charts, and graphs can be used to stimulate discussion about aspects of what is depicted and to encourage students to predict what the text is likely to be about.
- **Short-term direct experiences** Quick activities and questions about students' experiences provide opportunities for students to observe science-related phenomena and can stimulate discussion of what students have observed. Teachers help students relate their observations or experiences to the content of the science lesson.
- **Long-term direct experiences** Class projects and formal inquiry activities provide an avenue for students to actively relate to abstract concepts.
- **Writing about what we know** Dialogue journals for note taking and responses to written prompts are useful means for the student to both record information and review it later.

2. Access Content

We can also support or *scaffold* students' learning by modifying the input itself. We provide this scaffolding by embedding the content in a richly redundant context with multiple routes to the meaning in addition to the language itself. Building this redundancy enables ESL students to access the content despite any limitations in English language proficiency.

Strategies that improve student access to academic content.

The following methods, which you will find embedded in Scott Foresman *Science*, can help students more effectively get access to meaning.

- **Use Visuals** Visuals enable students to "see" the basic concept we are trying to teach much more effectively than if we rely only on words. When students are reading science textbooks, we can systematically draw their attention to the importance of context and picture clues in figuring out the meaning. The Picture/Text Walk feature in Scott Foresman *Science* Every Student Learns Teacher's Guide draws attention to specific pictures and offers models of language the teacher can use to talk about those pictures with the students to clarify the meaning.

© Pearson Education, Inc. 3

- ***Dramatize/Act Out*** For beginning ESL students, *Total Physical Response*, where students physically represent a phenomenon or act out commands, can be highly effective.
- ***Clarify Language*** Language-oriented activities aim to clarify the meanings of new words and concepts. Teachers can modify their language by paraphrasing ideas and explaining new concepts and words. They explain new words by providing synonyms, antonyms, and definitions either in English or in the home language of students. Important vocabulary can be repeated and recycled as part of the paraphrasing of ideas. The meaning can also be communicated and/or reinforced through gestures, body language, and demonstrations.
- ***Make Personal and Cultural Connections*** Scripted questions in the Scott Foresman *Science* Every Student Learns Teacher's Guide suggest ways to link content to students' everyday experiences. These content connections validate students' sense of identity and make the learning more meaningful.
- ***Make Cross-Curricular Connections*** The more cognitive operations students perform related to a particular issue or problem, the deeper their comprehension becomes.
- ***Provide Hands-on Experiences*** The more we can contextualize or personalize abstract concepts by embedding them in students' hands-on experiences, the more comprehensible they will become for students. Hands-on projects also allow students to link the conversational language they use in the "real" world and the more abstract and specialized language they are learning in science. Discussions about concrete phenomena and problems demystify the language of science. The abstract concepts we learn in science help us understand what we see with our very own eyes and vice-versa.
- ***Encourage Learning Strategies*** Learning strategies are useful for all students, but particularly for ESL students who face obvious challenges in accessing curricular content. Examples of strategies included in Scott Foresman *Science* are: planning tasks or activities, visualization, grouping and classifying information, taking notes and summarizing information, questioning for clarification, and using multiple resources and reference materials to find information or complete a task.

3. Extend Language

A systematic focus on and exploration of language is essential if students are to develop knowledge of the specific vocabulary and text structures that are used in scientific discourse. Students can systematically collect the meanings of words and phrases they encounter in science texts in a personal or group *language bank*.

Strategies that help students accelerate their acquisition of academic language.

A variety of strategies to activate students' prior knowledge are embedded in Scott Foresman *Science*.

- **Explore Etymology** Paradoxically, the complexity of scientific language provides some important opportunities for language exploration. A large percentage of the less frequent academic and technical vocabulary of English derives from Latin and Greek roots. So word formation often follows some very predictable patterns.

- **Identify Rules and Conventions** When students know some of the rules or conventions of how academic words are formed, they have an edge in extending their vocabulary. It helps them not only figure out the meanings of individual words but also how to form different parts of speech from these words.

- **Relate Academic Words to Students' First Language** This encourages students to relate the English word to their prior knowledge of the word (or related words in their first language). It also provides students with an opportunity to display and feel proud of their first language linguistic expertise.

- **Identify and Practice Conjugates** When we demystify how academic language works, students are more likely to recognize parts of speech in their reading of complex text across the curriculum and to become more adept at inferring meanings from context. For example, the student who recognizes that *acceleration* is a noun (rather than a verb or adjective) has taken a step closer to the meaning of the term in the context of a particular sentence or text.

- **Model Appropriate Academic Language** If teachers provide good models, then students can extend their own command of more formal registers of language. In addition, students must be given the opportunity and incentive to use academic language in both oral and written modalities.

Conclusion

Science will assume relevance to students and be learned much more effectively when students can relate the content of instruction to their prior experience and current interests. In addition to activating students' prior knowledge and building background knowledge, we may need to modify our instruction in specific ways to make the content accessible to ESL students who are still in the process of catching up to native-speakers in academic English language proficiency.

These supports should focus not only on making the scientific content comprehensible to students but also on extending their awareness of how the language of science works. In this way, students can develop insights about academic language that will bear fruit in other areas. When we integrate these active uses of language with the science curriculum, students benefit both with respect to their knowledge of scientific content and language abilities.

References

Chamot, A. U. & O'Malley, J.M. (1994). *The CALLA Handbook: Implementing the Cognitive Academic Language Learning Approach.* Reading, MA: Addison-Wesley.

Collier, V. P. and Thomas, W. P. (1999). Making U.S. schools effective for English language learners, Part 1. *TESOL Matters*, 9:4 (August/September), pp. 1 & 6.

Cummins (2001). *Negotiating identities: Education for empowerment in a diverse society. 2nd edition.* Los Angeles: California Association for Bilingual Education.

Díaz-Rico, L. & Weed, K. Z. (2002). *The crosscultural, language, and academic development handbook: A complete K-12 reference guide. 2nd edition.* Boston: Allyn & Bacon.

Gibbons, P. (1991). *Learning to learn in a second language.* Newtown, Australia: Primary English Teaching Association.

Meyer, L. (2000). Barriers to meaningful instruction for English learners. *Theory into Practice, 34*(2), 228-236.

Neuman, S. B. (1999). Books make a difference: A study of access to literacy. *Reading Research Quarterly, 34*(3), 286-311.

Schmitt, N. (2000). *Vocabulary in language teaching.* Cambridge, UK: Cambridge University Press.

🎯Compare and Contrast

Look at the pictures of the seedling and the adult plant. Study the graphic organizer to see how the two plants are different and how they are alike.

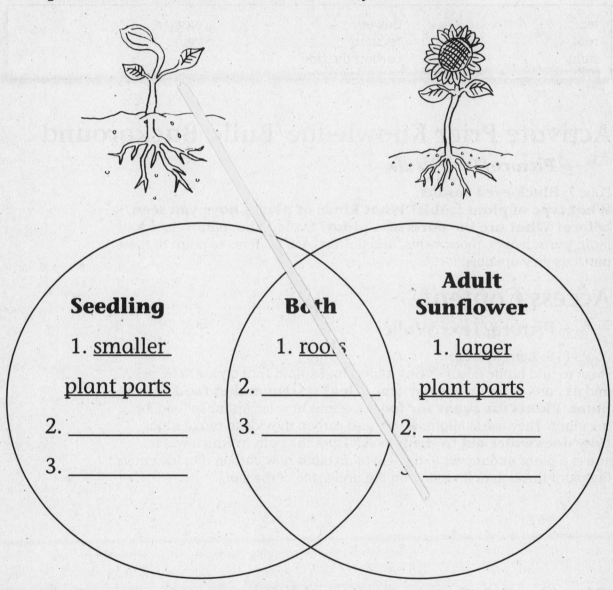

Seedling

1. smaller

plant parts

2. _____

3. _____

Both

1. roots

2. _____

3. _____

Adult Sunflower

1. larger

plant parts

2. _____

3. _____

Read each item. Decide where it belongs in the organizer above. Write one letter on each line.

A. has no flower   D. is short
B. has leaves   E. has a stem
C. is tall   F. has a flower

Lesson 1: What are the main parts of a plant?

Vocabulary

leaf	flower	oxygen
root	*system	vein
stem	carbon dioxide	

Activate Prior Knowledge/Build Background

 **Picture/Text Walk**

Page 7: **Black-eyed Susans**
What type of plant is this? What kinds of plants have you seen before? What are the parts of a plant? Explain that plants have four main parts: leaves, roots, stems, and flowers. Ask students to point to these parts, as they are able.

Access Content

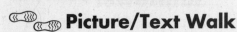 **Picture/Text Walk**

Pages 8–9: **Leaf system**
Point to and name a leaf's veins and stem. Explain that a plant's leaves and its parts make up a leaf system. **A leaf system makes food for the plant. Plants use sugar for food.** Explain how leaves make food for the plant. They use sunlight, water, and carbon dioxide to make sugar. **How does water get to the leaves?** Trace the path in which water enters a plant and moves to the leaves. Explain how carbon dioxide enters the plant through holes found on the underside of the leaf.

Picture It! Compare and Contrast

Have students look at the pictures to compare how the two plants are alike and different. Point out to students how they can organize information on the graphic organizer to compare and contrast. Explain that this organizer, called a Venn diagram, has two overlapping parts. The left part tells about one thing; the right part tells about another thing. The part in the middle tells how the two things are similar. Discuss the first numbered item in each section. Then have students complete the organizer.

Lesson 2: Why do plants need roots and stems?

Vocabulary

root
taproot

root hairs
tubes

Activate Prior Knowledge/Build Background

Give groups of students small jars filled with water and lengths of different absorbent materials, such as sponges or thick string. Encourage students to dip one end of each material into the water. Ask students to observe what happens to the water and to the material.

Access Content

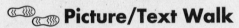 **Picture/Text Walk**

Page 10: **Roots**
Point to the pine tree. **Where are the roots?** Trace the path in which water travels from the base of the roots to the top of the tree.

Page 11: **Roots that we eat**
Point to the carrot pictured. Explain that carrots have one large root called a taproot. There are tiny hairs, called root hairs, at the tips of these roots. They absorb water for the plant. Poin t to the other roots pictured. Invite students to name them. **Have you eaten any of these roots?**

Page 11: **Grass**
Point to the clump of grass pictured. **Does this grass have a taproot?**

Page 12: **Cactus stem diagram**
Remind students that a plant's stem supports its leaves, flowers, and fruits. Explain that stems have tubes that move water and minerals from a plant's roots to its leaves. Point to the diagram. **This is a cactus stem. The stem becomes bigger when it takes in water. What do you think happens to the stem when the cactus uses up the water?**

Lesson 3: How are plants grouped?

Vocabulary

*deciduous	seeds	*coniferous
petals	*pollinate	cones
pollen	flower	

Activate Prior Knowledge/Build Background

 Picture/Text Walk

Page 14: Flowering tree and flowering trillium
Point to the tree. **What is this?** Point to the trillium. Explain that it is
an herb, a kind of plant. **How are the tree and herb alike? How are
they different?**

Access Content

 Picture/Text Walk

Page 15: Bee and flower
**This is a flower. Flowers make pollen or seeds. Do all plants
have flowers?** Explain that plants can be grouped by whether they have
flowers or cones.

Pages 16–17: Two kinds of cones
**These trees are called coniferous trees. Do coniferous trees have
flowers?** (no) Instead, coniferous trees grow cones to make their seeds.
Coniferous trees make two kinds of cones. They make pollen cones;
they also make seed cones.

Extend Language

Write and say the words *petal/pedal.* These words sound the same but have
different meanings. We use the noun *petal* to describe a plant part. *Pedal*
can be used as both a noun and a verb. Invite students to help you make
a sentence using each word. Practice the same exercise with the words
wood and *would.*

© Pearson Education, Inc. 3

Sequence

A Frog's Life Cycle

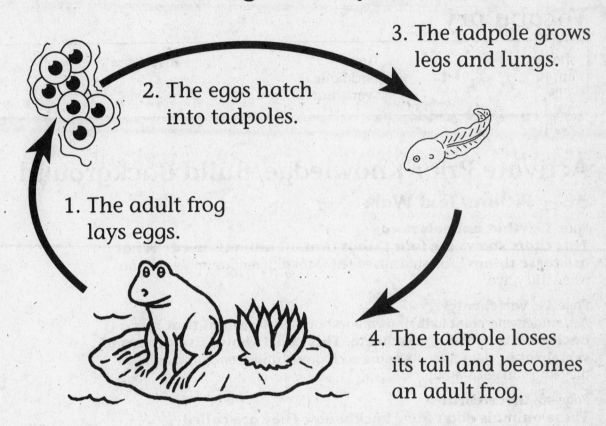

3. The tadpole grows legs and lungs.

2. The eggs hatch into tadpoles.

1. The adult frog lays eggs.

4. The tadpole loses its tail and becomes an adult frog.

A frog changes a lot during its life cycle. The steps happen in sequence from first to last.

Look at these steps from the life cycle of a frog. They are **not** in the correct sequence. Write the correct number next to each step.

_____3_____ The tadpole grows legs and lungs.

_____ The adult frog lays eggs.

_____ The eggs hatch into tadpoles.

_____ The tadpole loses its tail and becomes an adult frog.

Lesson 1: How are animals grouped?

Vocabulary

shelter	*trait	invertebrate
lungs	backbone	
gills	*vertebrate	

Activate Prior Knowledge/Build Background

Picture/Text Walk

Page 39: **What animals need**
This chart shows the four things that all animals need. What are these things? Ask students to tell what different animals eat and where they live.

Page 41: **Vertebrates**
Ask students to point to their own backbones. **An animal that has a backbone is called a vertebrate. This chart shows five groups of vertebrates.** Help students name each group and then name animals they know in each group.

Page 43: **Invertebrates**
These animals don't have backbones. They are called invertebrates. Which animals have a hard shell? Which animals have no hard parts? Help students name the animals pictured in the chart.

Access Content

Have groups of students pick either the chart that shows vertebrates or the chart that shows invertebrates. Ask them to pantomime the movement of two of these animals, using their hands or their whole bodies. The other students guess the name of the animal and say whether it is a vertebrate or an invertebrate.

Picture It! Sequence

Explain to students that *sequence* is the order in which things happen. **An animal's life cycle is how the animal grows and changes during its life. Things happen in a certain order. For example, the animal must grow before it becomes an adult.** Guide students as they review the life cycle of the frog. Help students to order the stages of a frog's life at the bottom of the page.

Every Student Learns

Lesson 2: How do animals grow and change?

Vocabulary

egg	caterpillar	tadpole
*larva	butterfly	frog
*pupa	amphibian	mammal

Activate Prior Knowledge/Build Background

Explain that the life cycle of an animal starts when it is born and ends when it dies. Invite students to describe the life cycle of an animal they know, such as a dog.

Access Content

👣 Picture/Text Walk

Pages 44–45: The life cycle of a butterfly
Ask students to repeat the stages of the life cycle after you say them. Then, ask students to identify the pictures of the caterpillar, egg and adult buttefly. **How do adult butterflies start a new life cycle?** (They lay eggs.) **Is the egg big or small? What comes out of the egg? What does the caterpillar turn into? What happens next?** Help students apply the stages of the life cycle to the pictures.

Pages 46–47: The life cycle of a frog
Point to the frog. Tell students that a frog is a kind of amphibian. It is a vertebrate. Explain that amphibians go through big changes as they become adults. Discuss Stage 1. **A mother frog can lay thousands of eggs. Are these eggs on dry land or in the water?** Point to Stage 2. **A tadpole lives underwater. It breathes with gills.** Point to Stage 3. Ask students to identify the physical differences between the tadpole in Stage 2 and the tadpole in Stage 3. Be sure to mention that to be an adult, the tadpole must grow lungs so that it can breathe on land. Point to Stage 4. **Have you ever seen an adult frog? Where do frogs live?**

Extend Language

Point to one of the life cycle diagrams and ask students why its movement can be compared to a circle or wheel. Tell students that the word *cycle* can also mean "wheel." Write the words *unicycle, bicycle,* and *tricycle.* Underline *cycle* in each word. Explain that a unicycle has one wheel, a bicycle has two wheels, and a tricycle has three wheels.

Lesson 3: How do adaptations help animals?

Vocabulary

*adaptation	teeth	*migrate
*inherited	bill	*hibernate
skull	protect	

Activate Prior Knowledge/Build Background

Ask students to name some things people can do using their fingers and thumbs. **How do our hands help us to do things?** Then have them mention another animal. **What does the animal do with its hands (paws, feet)?** Have groups of students compare the mouth or teeth of two animals they know. **What does each animal eat? How does its mouth and teeth help it eat its food?**

Access Content

Picture/Text Walk

Page 48: **Porcupine and hyena skulls**
Explain that animals have adaptations that help them to survive in their environments. Lead students in examining the teeth of both the porcupine skull and the hyena skull. **Which animal has teeth to eat plants?** (porcupine) **Which animal has teeth to eat meat?** (hyena)

Page 49: **Different bills**
Help students identify the bill of each bird. **This bird is a pelican. The pelican has a bill that helps it catch fish in the water.** Invite students to point to birds as you say the names. Then, help them describe each bill and what it is used for. **Which bird is the cardinal? The cardinal has a short, strong bill to help it open seeds.**

Page 50: **Porcupine protection**
Explain that animals protect themselves in many different ways. **This is a porcupine. What do you think this porcupine does to protect itself?**

Page 52: **Instincts**
Instincts are behaviors that animals can do when they are born. What are these animals doing that are instincts? Invite students to name the animals and tell what they are doing.

Lesson 4: How are animals from the past like today's animals?

Vocabulary

tree sap	lizard
amber	dinosaur

Activate Prior Knowledge/Build Background

〰️〰️ Picture/Text Walk

Pages 54–55: **Dinosaur skull**
Point to the skull. **This is the skull of a dinosaur. Are dinosaurs still alive today? Why not?**

Page 54: **Fossils**
Explain that the trilobite is extinct; it no longer lives on Earth. **This is a picture of trilobite fossil. Fossils are signs of plants or animals that lived long ago.** Point out that a fossil is not made of actual animal parts; most fossils are made of rock.

Access Content

Page 55: **A very old spider**
Explain that this spider lived millions of years ago. It got stuck in tree sap. Then the sap turned hard like a rock after many years. Point to the picture of the saber-toothed tiger fossil. **How do you think this tiger turned into a fossil?**

Pages 56–57: **The Badlands, today and long ago**
Point to the picture of the *Tyrannosaurus rex*. **The *T. rex* was a dinosaur that lived on Earth long ago.** Ask students to describe the habitat that surrounds it. Explain that the Badlands were hot and wet when the dinosaurs lived there. Then, the climate changed; it may have become much cooler. Dinosaurs did not adapt to this new climate. As a result, they became extinct. Point to the picture of the Badlands today. **How are the Badlands different today?** Explain that the climate is hot and dry. Only animals that are adapted to these conditions can live there now.

Extend Language

Talk about the word *extinct*. It is an adjective that means that something, such as a species of animal, does not live on Earth anymore. Explain that it comes from the same Latin word as extinguish, which means "to put out, end, destroy." Ask students to use the words in sentences. **What is another way to say, "We need to put out the fire?" What is another way to say, "Dinosaurs don't live on earth any more?"**

⟲ Main Idea and Details

You can use a word web to show the main idea and details of an article or lesson. The details give information about the main idea. The main idea is in the center and the details are in the boxes.

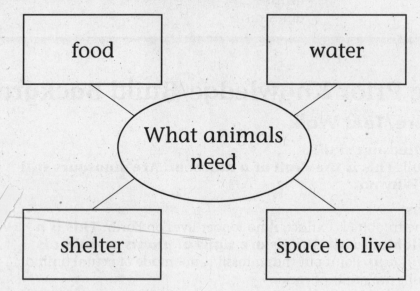

food

water

What animals need

shelter

space to live

N w fill in the word web below. Use *Animals with ackbones* as your main idea. Write four details that are the names of animals with backbones.

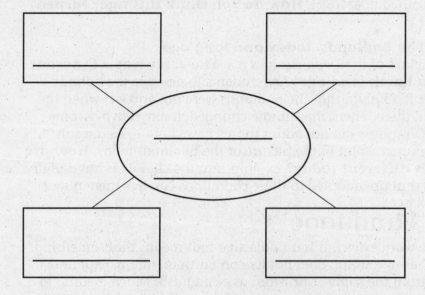

Lesson 1: What are ecosystems?

Vocabulary

*environment	*ecosystem	*community
climate	habitat	
interact	*population	

Activate Prior Knowledge/Build Background

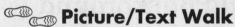 **Picture/Text Walk**

Pages 72–73: **Coastal environment**
Point to a tree. Ask students to identify both the living and nonliving parts that surround the tree. Explain that these parts make up the coastal environment pictured. The parts that depend on one another make up an ecosystem.

Access Content

Pages 74–75: **Coyotes and chaparral**
Ask students to point to the coyote. Explain that coyotes live in an environment similar to that pictured on page 75. **All the coyotes that live here at the same time make up a population.**

Page 75: **Ground squirrels**
Have a volunteer point to the ground squirrel. Explain that the ground squirrel lives in the same environment as the coyote. The population of both animals that live in this environment make up a community.

Picture It! Main Idea and Details

Explain that a main idea is a "big idea." Every main idea has ideas that are a part of that idea. These are called *details*. **For example, if our main idea is "Parts of the body," what could be some details?** Elicit responses from students. Review the main idea and details graphic organizer to be sure that students understand it. Provide assistance as required as students complete the graphic organizer, "Animals with backbones."

Use with pages 76–81.

Lesson 2: Which ecosystems have few trees?

Vocabulary

*grassland	*desert	winter
roots	*tundra	snow

Activate Prior Knowledge/Build Background

Ask students to describe the climate where you live. Make a list of words and phrases that describe the temperatures and yearly amounts of rain or snowfall. Then, ask students to describe the kinds of plants that are able to survive in this climate.

Access Content

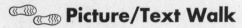 **Picture/Text Walk**

Page 77: **Grassland**
What kinds of plants do you see in this picture? Are there many trees? This is a grassland. A grassland is an ecosystem; it has cold winters and hot summers. Point out the grasses and flowering plants. Explain that they can survive in the grassland because they have deep roots. **Deep roots help the plants find water during the dry, hot summers.**

Pages 78–79: **Desert**
What is this ecosystem called? This is a desert. It is hot during the day and cold at night. What are some plants and animals that live here? Discuss that many desert animals escape to cooler places during the day. Be sure to point out how some plants have adapted to allow them to live in this environment. For example, cactuses can store water in their leaves and stems.

Pages 80–81: **Tundra**
What kinds of plants and animals do you see here? Point out the snow on the mountaintops. **What do you think the climate is like here?** Explain that the tundra is cold and dry.

© Pearson Education, Inc. 3

Every Student Learns

Lesson 3: Forests—many kinds

Vocabulary

coniferous	deciduous	tropical
needles	forest	equator

Activate Prior Knowledge/Build Background

Ask students to describe different kinds of forests they have walked
in or seen. Have them describe the location and climate of each forest.
Then, ask them to describe the trees, plants, and animals that lived in
each forest.

Access Content

Picture/Text Walk

Page 83: **Coniferous and deciduous forests**
Which of these forests has trees with needles? Point to the
coniferous forest; explain that it is found in places that have cold, snowy
winters. The conifers' leaves, or needles, are intended to withstand the
weight of the snow. Then, point to the picture of the deciduous forest. **Do
these trees have needles?** Ask students why they don't have needles.
Explain that it is because deciduous trees grow in places that are generally
warmer than those of coniferous forests.

Pages 84–85 **Tropical forests**
**This is a picture of a tropical forest. Do you think a tropical
forest gets a lot of rain? Why?**

Extend Language

Point to the picture of the beaver on page 83. Discuss how people are
compared to animals. Write the phrase *busy as a beaver* on the chalkboard.
Explain that because beavers do a lot of work, we say that someone who
works a lot is as "busy as a beaver." Help students make sentences with
other phrases, such as *quiet as a mouse, big as a bear, strong as an ox.*

Lesson 4: What are water ecosystems?

Vocabulary

freshwater	river	salt marsh
saltwater	stream	oceans
lake	springs	
pond	*wetland	

Activate Prior Knowledge/Build Background

Ask students if they have ever been to a beach. Ask them if they swam in the water. **Was the water salty?** Explain that oceans have saltwater. Ask students to contemplate the kinds of water bodies that hold freshwater.

Access Content

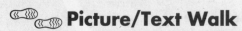 **Picture/Text Walk**

Pages 86–87: **Freshwater ecosystems**
This bird is standing in a wetland. What do you think a wetland is? Explain that a wetland is part of a freshwater ecosystem. Ask students where they think freshwater comes from. Discuss how most lakes and rivers get their water from rain or melting snow. Then, point to the picture of the Weeki Wachee River on page 87. Explain that its freshwater comes from a spring underground.

Pages 88–89: **Saltwater ecosystems**
Point to the coral reef on page 89. Explain that an ocean is also a water ecosystem. **Ocean water contains salt. There are many rivers that flow into the ocean. The river's freshwater mixes with the ocean's saltwater. This area can form into a salt marsh.** Explain that salt marshes are wetlands. Special animals live in salt marshes. They can live in salty water and soil.

Extend Language

Point out to students that the word *spring* can be used as a noun and as a verb. A *spring* is a place where water *springs* from underground. Write the words *water* and *swim* on the chalkboard. Help students to use each word as a noun in one sentence and as a verb in another.

© Pearson Education, Inc. 3

🎯 Draw Conclusions

You can use facts you know or learn to create a new idea, or a conclusion. Study the graphic organizer below. Think about how the facts support the conclusion.

Plants need space to grow.	
Fires can burn away plants.	Fires can help new plants grow.
Ash from fires are good for plants.	

Now, read the phrases below. Three phrases are facts and one phrase is a conclusion. Write each fact in a box on the left. Write the conclusion in the box on the right.

1. Grass grows on the prairie.
2. Mice eat the grass.
3. Plants and animals are part of a food web.
4. Eagles eat the mice.

Lesson 1: How do living things interact?

Vocabulary

interact	herd

Activate Prior Knowledge/Build Background

Ask students where they can see groups of people. List students' responses on the board. Students might name a sports event, school, mall, park.) Point to each place listed. **What kinds of different things are people doing in this place?** Solicit that people are interacting in different ways (for example, at a sports event there may be athletes, spectators, vendors selling food, ticket-takers).

Access Content

 Picture/Text Walk

Page 103: **Living things interacting**
Point out to students that the chart shows three ways that living things interact. **How do members of a herd of animals help each other? How can they protect each other from other animals that hunt them? How can a tree help a flower get light? How do an insect and a flower help each other?**

Page 104: **Bees and barnacles**
When one bee finds some flowers, what does it do to help the other bees in the beehive? Explain that these barnacles eat food from the water that the whale swims through. **How does the whale help the barnacles?**

Page 105: **The cleaner fish**
This is a cleaner fish. It eats small, harmful animals off the big fish. How do the big fish and the little fish help each other?

Picture It! Draw Conclusions

Have students study the facts and conclusion in the first graphic organizer. Discuss how the facts lead to the conclusion. Then read aloud the directions for the students' activity. Point out that three of the phrases are facts, and one phrase is a conclusion that can be made from those facts. After students identify each phrase as a fact or a conclusion, have them fill in the organizer. Remind students that a conclusion is supported by the facts.

© Pearson Education, Inc. 3

Lesson 2: How do living things get energy?

Vocabulary

energy	*herbivores	*prey
*producers	*carnivores	*predator
*consumers	*omnivores	food web

Activate Prior Knowledge/Build Background

Write the following three headings on the board: Eats Plants/Eats Animals/Eats Plants and Animals. **What animals eat plants? What animals eat meat? What animals eat both plants and other animals?** List students' responses under the correct headings. **What do people eat?**

Access Content

🐚🐚🐚 Picture/Text Walk

Page 106: **Producers and Consumers**
Explain that plants are called producers because they make their own food. **Where is the producer in this picture?** Explain that a consumer eats food to get energy. **Where is the consumer in this picture?** Point out that all energy begins with the Sun.

Page 107: **Three kinds of consumers**
Discuss how each of these consumers gets energy. **Does a raccoon eat plants, meat, or both plants and meat?** Explain that consumers that eat plants and meat are called omnivores. **Sheep are herbivores. What do they eat? A wolf is a carnivore. What do wolves eat? Do carnivores eat plants?**

Page 108: **Food webs**
What is the producer in this diagram? What are the consumers? Does the energy go from the mice to the grass or from the grass to the mice? Explain that golden eagles eat mice. Eagles are predators and mice are prey. **What would happen to the eagles if the mouse population got smaller?** Point out that energy from the grass flows to the different consumers. Remind students that the prairie grass needs sunlight to grow. All food webs start with the energy from the Sun.

Lesson 3: How do living things compete?

Vocabulary

compete	*competition	resource

Activate Prior Knowledge/Build Background

Have students discuss sports competitions they have seen. Ask them to describe how many people were in each competition, what the rules were, how a person or team won each competition, and what happened to the winners and losers. Ask them to describe other ways that people compete with each other.

Access Content

Picture/Text Walk

Page 110: **Competing for different resources**
The trees in the top picture compete for space. What else do they compete for? What are the animals in the bottom picture competing for? What will happen if there is not enough water for all of them?

Page 111: **Lion, hyenas, and prey**
What are the lion and the hyenas competing for in this picture?

Page 113: **A cycle of competition**
Explain that the green bars on the graph show how much grass there is during four years on the tundra. The purple bars show the lemming population. **Was there a lot of grass for the lemmings to eat in the first year? What happened to the lemming population in the second and third years? Why did the lemming population get smaller again in the fourth year?**

Extend Language

Review the meaning of the words *predator* and *prey* with students. Write each word on an index card. Show them three to five pairs of pictures of animals that are predator and prey, for example, a lion and a gazelle, a frog and a fly, or a snake and a frog. Have students take turns matching the index cards to the animals in each pair of pictures.

Lesson 4: How do environments change?

Vocabulary

dam	flood	*decomposer
natural	drought	*decay
events	volcano	

Activate Prior Knowledge/Build Background

Provide students with a tray full of sand, water, tools to move the sand around, and a container in which they can store sand. Ask them to work in small groups to change this environment in different ways. After each group has changed the sand environment, have them explain what they did. Ask them what forces might make these kind of changes happen in the natural world.

Access Content

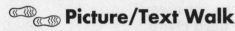 **Picture/Text Walk**

Pages 114–115: **Changes in the environment**
What are some ways these pictures show environments changing? Which changes were caused by natural events? Which changes were caused by animals?

Page 117: **Fire and plants**
What are some ways that plants can get burned? What happens after a fire is over? How does fire help new plants grow?

Pages 118–119: **Living and decaying trees**
Explain that decomposers are living things that break down things that have died. This is called decay. **What are some living things in these pictures? What decomposers do you see? Why are the small trees in the bottom picture growing in the old log of the dead tree?**

Extend Language

Write the word *decompose*. Explain that the *de-* at the beginning is a suffix. It means "to do the opposite of" or "remove." The opposite of *compose*, "to put together," is *decompose*, "to break down." Ask students to explain the meaning of these words: *decode, defrost, decontrol,* and *desalt.*

Lesson 5: What is a healthy environment for people?

Vocabulary

garbage	digestive juices	large intestine
stomach	small intestine	healthy

Activate Prior Knowledge/Build Background

Have students work with partners to make a list of what people need to live. Call on partners to present their lists to the class to compare responses. Use students' lists to create a list on the board.

Access Content

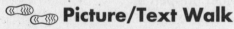 Picture/Text Walk

Page 121: **Things people need**
These pictures show the basic things people need to live. **Where does our water come from? Does our food come from near or far away? Describe the place where you live. Why do people need clean air? Where does our garbage go when we throw it out?**

Pages 122–123: **Food turns into energy**
How do we get the energy our bodies need? Point to the picture of different foods. **What are some different kinds of food that we should eat to stay healthy? What are some ways that we keep these foods clean and fresh? How does our body get energy from food?** Use the illustration to trace how food is digested and gives the body energy.

Extend Language

Review with students the mouth, stomach, small intestine, and large intestine. Have them point to where each is in their own body. Then, ask them to name other parts of the body, including parts that are on the inside and the outside. Make a list of these words. Help students tell what each part does and how it works.

© Pearson Education, Inc. 3

Lesson 6: How can people stay healthy?

Vocabulary

exercise	circulatory system	*disease
heart	*germs	microscope
lungs	bacteria	
muscles	virus	

Activate Prior Knowledge/Build Background

What are some ways you can get exercise? Why is exercise important? How does exercise help keep bodies healthy? You may wish to have students place their hands over their heart to feel their heartbeat. Then ask them to jump up and down ten times, and then feel their heartbeat. Do they notice a difference? How so?

Access Content

 **Picture/Text Walk**

Pages 124–125: **Exercise, blood, and oxygen**
Point to the circulatory system. Explain that it moves blood through the body. Name some parts of the circulatory system. Point to the respiratory system. Explain that it brings oxygen into the body. **What are some parts of the respiratory system?**

Pages 126–127: **Germs and disease**
If you look through the microscope, you can see these three kinds of germs. Explain that germs like bacteria and viruses can cause diseases. **What are some diseases that germs cause?** Refer students to the rules on page 127. **What are some ways you can stop germs from spreading? How is each rule a good idea to help stop the spread of germs?**

Extend Language

Explain that *micro* means "enlarging or amplifying." What does a microscope do? (It magnifies objects that are too small to see with the naked eye.)

🎯 Cause and Effect

A cause makes something happen. An effect is what happens. Read the sentences below.

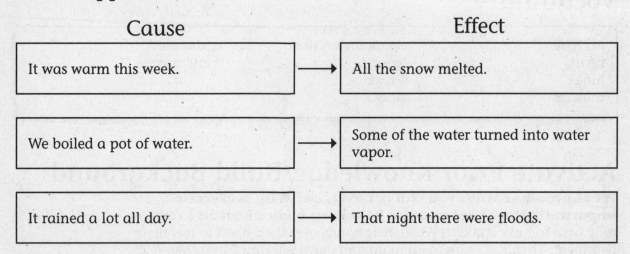

Cause		Effect
It was warm this week.	→	All the snow melted.
We boiled a pot of water.	→	Some of the water turned into water vapor.
It rained a lot all day.	→	That night there were floods.

Read the sentences below. Three sentences are causes. One sentence is the effect. Write the three causes in the boxes on the left. Write the effect in the box on the right.

1. Farmers water their crops.
2. Farmers plant seeds to grow crops.
3. We can buy fruits and vegetables to eat.
4. Trucks bring fruits and vegetables to stores.

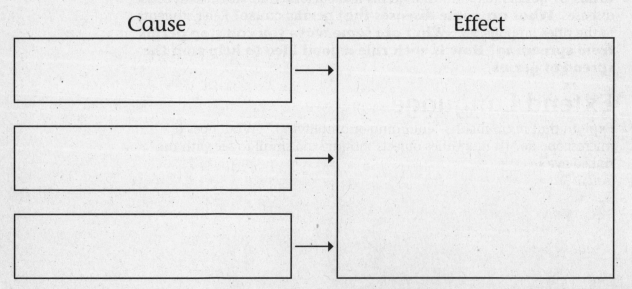

Cause		Effect
	→	
	→	
	→	

Making Inferences

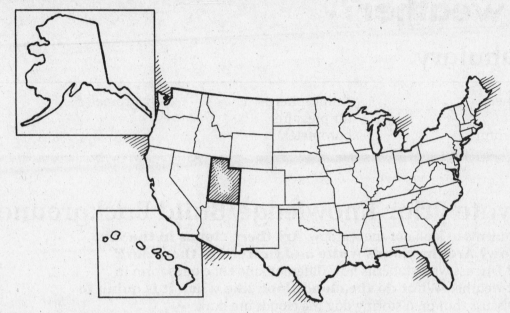

Find the weather for your area. What is the
weather like? Is there high (H) or low (L) pressure?
How do you think air pressure affects weather?
Make inferences based on facts from the map.

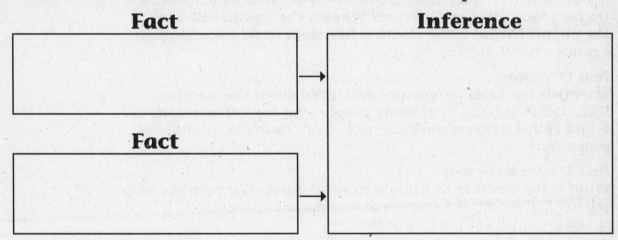

Fact		**Inference**
	→	
Fact		
	→	

Lesson 1: What makes up weather?

Vocabulary

*weather	*atmosphere	hygrometer
predict	air pressure	
temperature	barometer	

Activate Prior Knowledge/Build Background

Invite students to look out the window. **Are there clouds in the sky right now? Are the clouds white and fluffy? Are there dark clouds?** Discuss with students how different kinds of clouds form in different weather. **What do the clouds look like when it is going to rain?** Discuss that on a stormy day the clouds are dark.

Access Content

 Picture/Text Walk

Page 175: **Clouds**
Ask students to compare the clouds in the sky to the clouds in the picture. **Do they look alike or different? What is the weather like in the picture? What is the weather like right now?** Ask students to describe a recent storm in your area.

Page 177: **Tools**
Scientists use tools to measure and learn about the weather. Discuss what each tool does. **Many people who are not scientists use a tool called a thermometer.** Explain that a thermometer measures temperature.

Page 178: **Weather map**
What is the weather like in our area? What does a weather map tell us? Explain that the numbers show temperature. The letters "H" and "L" indicate high and low air pressure.

Picture It! Making Inferences

Help students find your area on the map. **What is the weather like in our area?** Point out that "H" means *high air pressure*, and "L" means *low air pressure*. Help students make the inference that high pressure usually signals clear or partly cloudy skies; low pressure usually means precipitation. Ask students to write these facts and inferences in the graphic organizer.

© Pearson Education, Inc. 3

Every Student Learns

Lesson 2: How does weather affect people?

Vocabulary

*hurricane	watch	patterns
*tornado	warning	desert
*blizzard	flood	

Activate Prior Knowledge/Build Background

Point out your region of the country on a map. Talk about the annual weather conditions where you live. **Do we get a lot of rain? Is it very hot in the summer?** Invite children to write about the weather and seasons in your area. Then, discuss the weather in other regions. Talk about an area that usually gets a lot of rain, such as the Northwest, and an area that is hot in the summer, such as the Southwest. **Weather is different because of weather patterns.**

Access Content

☜☞ Picture/Text Walk

Page 180: **Weather patterns**
Point to the chart. The chart shows two different weather patterns for the state of Washington. **The western part of the state is near the ocean. Places near the ocean usually get more rain than places away from the ocean. What does the chart tell us about the temperatures in each part of the state?** Invite students to talk about different weather in places they have been.

Pages 180–181: **Sonoran Desert**
All deserts are dry. Not all deserts are alike. Explain that the Sonoran Desert gets a lot of rainfall during the summer. Point out the Sonoran Desert on a map. Show that it gets moisture from the Gulf of California.

Page 182: **Dangerous storms**
Explain that a hurricane has strong winds and heavy rain. A tornado is spinning air. A blizzard is a winter storm. **How are they alike? How are they different?** Explore ways to stay safe during these storms.

Extend Language

Write the names *Sonoran Desert* and *Gulf of California*. Pronounce each name. Circle the beginning letter of each word. Point out how each word begins with a capital letter. Explain that these are proper names, just like the first and last name of a person. **A proper name begins with a capital letter.** Repeat using *Cascade Mountains* and *North America*.

Name _____

Compare and Contrast

Fill in the graphic organizer to show how these soils are alike and different.

This soil is sandy. It feels rough. The roots of plants may not have time to soak up water. Sandy soil does not hold water well.

This soil is silty. It holds water very well. It is easier to grow plants in silty soil.

Sandy soil   **Both**   **Silty soil**

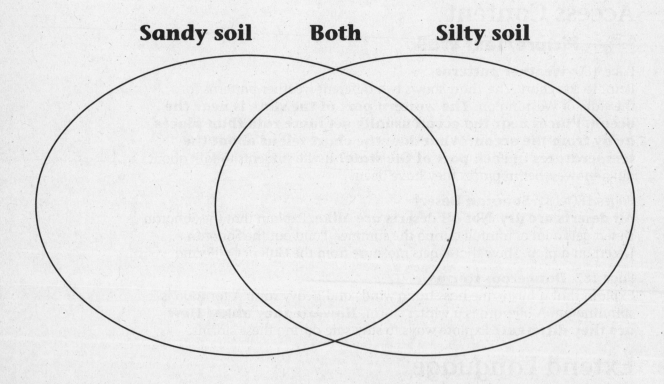

© Pearson Education, Inc. 3

Every Student Learns

Lesson 1: How do rocks form?

Vocabulary

*rock	sediment	extinct
*mineral	*sedimentary rock	*metamorphic rock
*igneous rock	fossil	

Activate Prior Knowledge/Build Background

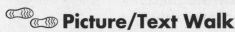 **Picture/Text Walk**

Page 199: **Mountains of rock**
What parts of this picture have rocks? Explain that rocks are found on mountains, along the ground, and in rivers, lakes, or streams. Ask students to point to the rocks in the picture. **What would it be like to walk on these rocks?**

Access Content

 **Picture/Text Walk**

Page 200: **Fossils in sedimentary rock**
Point to the word *sedimentary*. **What smaller word do you see in this word?** (sediment) Explain that animal and plant remains may become buried in *sediment* at the bottom of a stream. The mud and sand that make up the sediment may harden into rock over a long period of time. Fossils are the shape of plants or animals sometimes found in sedimentary rock. If the plants or animals no longer exist, they are extinct. **Have you seen fossils before? Where did you see them? What did they show?**

Page 201: **Rock groups**
What are the names of the main groups of rocks? Which groups can change? Which group has already changed? Remind students that both igneous and sedimentary rocks can become metamorphic rocks. Metamorphic rocks are igneous and sedimentary rocks that have been changed due to heat and pressure over a long period of time. Help students appreciate the time it takes rocks to form.

Picture It! Compare and Contrast

Invite students to look at the two pictures of soil. Before you read the captions, ask students to describe the color and consistency of each soil. Then, read the captions and point out the differences between the soils. **Which soil is better to have on a farm?** (silty) Help students complete the graphic organizer. (Possible answers: Sandy soil does not hold water well. Silty soil holds water well. Both are types of soil.)

Lesson 2: What are minerals

Vocabulary

magnet	luster

Activate Prior Knowledge/Build Background

Give groups of students a magnet and have them test the magnet on a variety of classroom objects. **What objects stick to the magnet?** Have students offer their own explanations of why certain objects stick to magnets while other objects do not. Explain that magnets come from the mineral magnetite. Magnets stick to anything made of iron, which is another kind of mineral.

Access Content

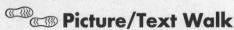 **Picture/Text Walk**

Page 203: **Properties of minerals**
Point to the entries on the chart for *mica*. **What is mica like?** Help students read each cell of the chart across the row. **Mica is black, gray, green, or violet. In light, it looks pearly (not very shiny).** Explain that different pieces of mica may make different kinds of streaks. **Mica is hard because you need a knife (rather than a coin or a fingernail) to scratch it.**

Page 204: **Minerals and health**
Have students work in small groups to cooperatively draw a picture of a meal made from foods that contain minerals identified in the text. Go from group to group and have students tell you about the minerals in their picture.

Page 205: **Minerals we use**
Which of these minerals did you use today? Remind students that minerals are a part of everyday life. You may wish to point out that all of the items that stuck to the magnets students experimented with earlier contained the mineral at the bottom of this chart: iron.

Lesson 3: Why is soil important?

Vocabulary

*soil	*decay	humus
topsoil	*nutrient	*loam
subsoil		

Activate Prior Knowledge/Build Background

Collect a sample of soil, taken either from outdoors or from a bag of gardening soil. Spread the soil out on newspaper and let students see it close up. **What color(s) do you see? What shapes? Is the soil wet or dry?** Explain that soil is a mixture of living and nonliving things.

Access Content

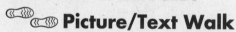 **Picture/Text Walk**

Page 206: **Living and nonliving material in soil**
Point out the earthworm in the soil. **What happens when earthworms die in the soil?** Explain that living things, like earthworms, breakdown, or decay, when they die. **After the earthworm dies and decays, it becomes a nutrient in the soil. Nutrients allow plants to grow.**

Page 207: **Soil layers**
Look at the topsoil layer. Point out that humus is made of living material that has decayed. Humus helps plants grow. Look at the next layer. **How is the subsoil different looking than the topsoil?** Point out the tree roots in the subsoil. Explain that water from rain or snow goes into this layer of soil. Remind students that roots help feed plants when they take in water. **In which layer do you find the most rock?** (The bottom layer of solid rock.)

Pages 208–209: **Loam**
What bits of rock can you find in different soils? (sand, clay, and/or silt) **What is loam made of?** (sand, silt, and clay; air, water, humus) Point out that loam is good soil to grow plants in.

Extend Language

What clue in the word *topsoil* helps you figure out which layer of soil it is (the word *top*). Explain that the prefix *sub-* means "below." **What clue in the word *subsoil* helps you figure out that subsoil is under *topsoil*?** (the prefix *sub-*, which means "below"). Discuss other examples such as *submarine* and *subterranean*.

⌖ Sequence

Glacier

The picture shows what a glacier can do. A glacier is a huge body of ice and snow. Write the sentences in the correct sequence in the correct box.

1. The glacier forms in cold places.
2. The glacier moves downhill.
3. Rocks line the edges where the glacier once stood.

First	**Next**	**Finally**

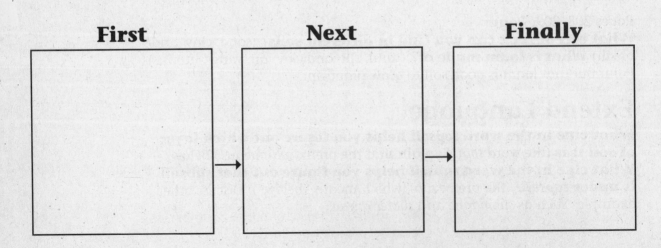

© Pearson Education, Inc. 3

Lesson 1: What are Earth's layers?

Vocabulary

*crust	*core
*mantle	*landform

Activate Prior Knowledge/Build Background

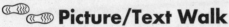 **Picture/Text Walk**

Pages 224–225: **Shapes on Earth's surface**
Which of these shapes do we have in our area? Help students point out and name the *landforms* or bodies of water that make up the region where you live. **Which of these landforms and bodies of water have you seen? Which would you like to see?**

Access Content

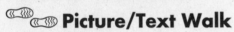 **Picture/Text Walk**

Page 223: **Earth's layers**
What does this diagram show? Explain that Earth, from its outside, or *crust,* down deep to its center, or *core,* is mostly made up of rock. To appreciate how thin or thick the layers of Earth are, suggest that students think about the layers in a basketball. A basketball often has a very thin skin on the outside—like Earth's crust. It has a somewhat thicker layer beneath the outer skin—like Earth's mantle. It has a very deep area, filled with air, which takes up the rest of the shape—like the Earth's core. **All of Earth's mountains, desserts, oceans, and other landforms are on Earth's crust.**

Extend Language

Write and say the word *core* and *crust.* These words have special meanings for science. They also have meanings that are not related to science. *Core* names the inner most layer of Earth. It also names the inner most section in certain kinds of fruit, like apples and pears. *Crust* names the outer most layer of Earth. It also names the outer layer of certain foods, such as pies.

Picture It! Sequence

Invite students to look at the picture of the glacier and describe what they see. Then, read the sequence of events aloud, pointing out relevant parts of the picture as you go. Explain that some things happen in a sequence or order of events. Help students fill out graphic organizer at the bottom of the page. Ask students to tell you the order of events from beginning to end.

Lesson 2: What are volcanoes and earthquakes?

Vocabulary

*magma	vibration	landslides
*lava	fault	

Activate Prior Knowledge/Build Background

Write and say the words *volcano* and *earthquake*. **Have you ever seen or felt a volcano or earthquake?** Allow children who have felt earthquakes or seen volcanoes describe their experience. Invite other children to tell what they know about volcanoes and earthquakes from movies, television, or books.

Access Content

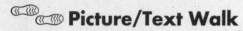 **Picture/Text Walk**

Page 227: **Volcanoes**
Why are there numbers in this picture? Help children understand that the events that cause a volcano take place in a certain order, or sequence. **Why is number 1 at the bottom of the page?** Explain that volcanoes begin with in Earth's mantle, where magma forms in chambers. The gases in magma push through weak rocks and cracks up into Earth's crust. The magma spills out from the volcano as lava and flows onto land and into bodies of water. Cooled lava can become igneous rock and grow into mountains.

Page 228: **Earthquakes**
Point to the cracks in the road. **These cracks happened when the earth shook, or vibrated in waves.** Help children understand that the vibrations in earthquakes happen when rocks in Earth's crust shift direction. This usually happens along a crack in Earth's crust, called a fault. The shifting in the crust causes shaking on land. The shaking land may cause buildings and roads to crack or crumble. Earthquakes also may cause very large waves to form in the ocean. or rocks and earth to slide down hills in a landslide.

Extend Language

Write and say the compound words earthquake and landslide. Then write the two words make up each compound: earth + quake and land + slide. Explain that each of these words is made up of two words that combine to form a new word. Explain how taking the compound word apart can sometimes help in understanding the new word. (quaking earth, sliding land)

© Pearson Education, Inc. 3

Every Student Learns

Lesson 3: What are weathering and erosion?

Vocabulary

*weathering	*erosion	gravity

Activate Prior Knowledge/Build Background

Write and say the word *weathering*. **What is the main word in weathering?** Explain that *weather* is a kind of action in Earth's atmosphere—like rain, snow, fog, or sunshine. Invite children to give examples of how the action of weather changes where they live, even if for a day. For example, rains may cause puddles or floods; snow may bury land and plants; too much sunshine and heat may dry up land.

Access Content

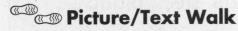 **Picture/Text Walk**

Page 230: **Weathering**
What kind of action does this picture show? Explain that *weathering* is an action. Living things that move or dig or mix up soil and plants whose roots grow into soil and rock may cause weathering. Water may cause weathering, also. **The action of weathering breaks rock into smaller pieces.**

Page 231: **Water and weathering**
When water freezes, it expands, or gets larger. Point out when water freezes and expands, it pushes against rock and can break the rock into smaller pieces. **Glaciers are made up of ice and snow, and they move slowly over Earth's crust.** Explain that the movement of glaciers causes weathering. The broken pieces of rock drop to the ground when a glacier melts.

Pages 232–233: **Erosion**
What allowed the hole in the cliff, the island, and the side of the hill to form? Help students understand that weathered material that moved helped to create these shapes and landforms. **Erosion is the movement of weathered material.** Read the captions for the first two pictures on page 232 to help students understand how water in the form of waves helped to move some weathered material. Have them look at the third picture. **Some of the material dropped and slid down because of *gravity*.** Have students look at the photograph on page 233. Read the caption aloud to help them understand how weathering and erosion shaped these rocks.

⟳Compare and Contrast

Read the words in the box below. Which describe renewable resources? Nonrenewable resources? Both? Write them in the correct section of the diagram.

Renewable Resource   Both   Nonrenewable Resource

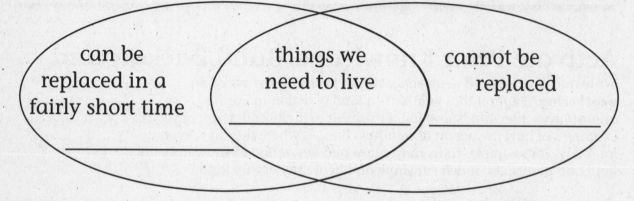

can be replaced in a fairly short time _____

things we need to live _____

cannot be replaced _____

coal, iron, oil
natural resources

water, air, trees, plants

Write each phrase below in the correct part of the diagram to show how farming and mining are alike and different.

planting crops
use machines to do work
use renewable resources,
  such as water, soil

dig for nonrenewable
  resources
use resources from Earth
provide fuel for cars

Farming   Both   Mining

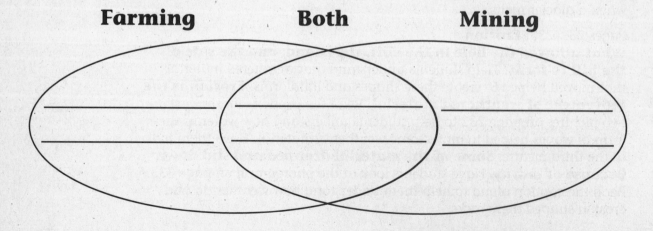

Lesson 1: What are resources?

Vocabulary

*natural resources	*renewable resource	*nonrenewable resource

Activate Prior Knowledge/Build Background

Explain that *resources* are materials. Natural resources are things that come from nature—Earth and the Sun. **Can you name some natural resources.**

Access Content

 Picture/Text Walk

Pages 246–247: **Renewable resources**
Where do logs come from? What are they used for? Explain that logs are the trunks of trees that have been cut down. Logs are an important building material. **What do people do to make sure they always will have logs as resources?** Explain that when people plant new trees, they make sure that logs and wood will be available in the future. **Renewable resources can be replaced in a fairly short period of time. Some resources are always available, like water, air, and sunlight.**

Page 249: **Nonrenewable resources**
Where does the coal come from? Point to the picture of the crane. **What is the crane doing?** Explain that we must dig coal from under the ground. Unlike a tree it cannot be planted or be replaced in a fairly short period of time. **What are some other nonrenewable resources?** Point out that many fuels come from nonrenewable resources, such as oil and natural gas. Building materials, such as steel, iron, copper, and aluminum, are nonrenewable resources.

Extend Language

Write and say the words *renewable* and *nonrenewable*. The prefix *re-* means "again," and the prefix *non-* means "not." The suffix *-able* means "can be." *Renewable* means "able to be new again." *Nonrenewable* means "cannot be new again."

Picture It! Compare and Contrast

Explain the difference between renewable and nonrenewable resources. Give examples of each. Help students to decide which phrases belong in each category of the Venn diagram. Provide guidance as necessary as they complete the Venn diagram.

Lesson 2: How can we protect our resources?

Vocabulary

*conservation	landfill

Activate Prior Knowledge/Build Background

Where does water come from? How do you use water every day at home, at school, and when you play? Explain that even though water is a resource with an endless supply, people need enough clean water to use and drink every day. **What can you do to help use water wisely and practice conservation?** Help children understand that people should use only the water they need to clean, cook, or drink.

Access Content

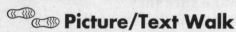 **Picture/Text Walk**

Page 250–251: **Conservation**
Point to the photo of the Florida wetland. Explain that the water in the wetland is being used again and again. The wetlands clean the water. Point to the picture of the farm. **The soil on the farm is used for planting many times. Recycling and cleaning up resources are ways people practice *conservation*—the wise use of resources. What other natural resource do people need to protect and keep clean?** Explain that air also needs to be used wisely and kept clean.

Pages 252–253: **Trash**
How do some of the things shown on the chart become trash?
Point out that the chart shows what most people throw away as trash, and the average amount of each thing that most people throw away. For example, when a plastic container of milk is empty, people may throw the plastic container away. An old newspaper may be thrown away. The trash is taken to an area of land and dumped or buried. That area of land is called a landfill. Point to the picture on page 253. **How can we make less trash? Can we use some of these things again?**

© Pearson Education, Inc. **3**

Every Student Learns

Lesson 3: What are ways to use resources again?

Vocabulary

*recycle

Activate Prior Knowledge/Build Background

Bring in a plastic milk jug or glass bottle and show it to students. **Can you think of ways to reuse a plastic milk jug (glass bottle)?** Allow students to share any ideas. **When we use something again**, we **conserve resources.** Ask students other ways of reusing things. (using jars and boxes, giving toys and clothing to others) Hold up the jug or bottle. **We can make new things out of old things. This is called recycling. What things do you think we can recycle?**

Access Content

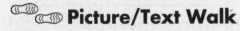 **Picture/Text Walk**

Pages 254–255: **Recycling glass**
Explain that each picture shows a step in the recycling process of glass. The process begins with glass jars or bottles that have already been used and thrown away. The process ends when the old jars or bottles are turned into new jars or bottles.

Pages 256–257: **Recycled products**
Products made from metal, glass, plastic, or paper can be recycled and turned into new products. Point to the photograph of the plastic park bench. **This bench was made from recycled plastic.** Point to the other photos and explain what they were made from. **What other things do you think could be made from recycled materials?**

Extend Language

Write and say the word *recycle*. Point to *re-*. *Re-* **is a prefix that means "again."** *Cycle* **means "things that keep happening."** *Recycle* **means "to bring something back again."**

Every Student Learns

Cause and the Effect

Study the graphic organizer below.

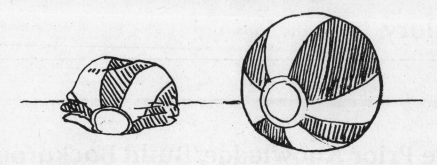

Cause		**Effect**
no air pumped into the ball, so no air pressure	→	ball does not bounce because gas particles of air do not push against one another
air pressure in ball from air pumped in	→	ball bounces because gas particles of air push up closely against one another under pressure

Fill in the graphic organizer. Remember: objects that have less density than water will float. Objects with more density will sink.

Cause		**Effect**
feather _____ _____	→	floats because _____ _____
rock _____ _____	→	sinks because _____ _____

Every Student Learns

Lesson 1: How can we describe matter?

Vocabulary

*matter	liquids	*atom
*property	*pressure	*periodic table
solids	*element	particles

Activate Prior Knowledge/Build Background

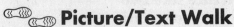 **Picture/Text Walk**

Page 279: **Matter**
Explain that everything we see, smell, and touch is *matter*. Even things we cannot see, smell, or touch—like air—are matter. **You learn about a property of matter by using your senses.**

Access Content

 **Picture/Text Walk**

Pages 280–281: **Forms of matter**
Which picture shows a solid? A liquid? A gas? Explain that solids keep their shape, while liquids take the shape of the container they are in, and gas has no shape.

Solids, liquids, and gas are made up of *particles*. Point out that particles in solids are very close and connected. They jiggle fast. Particles in liquids are loose and flow past each other. Particles in gas are not connected and bounce. Gas particles may or may not be pushed close to one another. The pushing is called *pressure*.

Page 282: **Parts of matter**
Take a piece of paper and cut it into pieces. Point out that the paper is made of particles. Explain that the paper may contain different kinds of particles. **Each different kind of particle is an *element*. The smallest particle of an element is called an *atom*.**

Page 283: **The periodic table**
The different elements are listed in the *periodic table*.

Picture It! Cause and Effect

Explain that the feather has less mass in same space as water; it floats because it is less dense than water. Rock has more mass; rock sinks because it is more dense than water.

Every Student Learns

Lesson 2: How are properties of matter measured?

Vocabulary

*mass   *volume   *density   *buoyancy

Activate Prior Knowledge/Build Background

 **Picture/Text Walk**

Page 284: **The Balance Scale and Mass**
How are the objects on the balance scale in the picture like two people on a seesaw? Explain a balance scale and a seesaw show which object weighs more. *Mass* is the amount of matter an object has.

Access Content

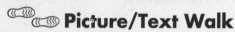 **Picture/Text Walk**

Page 285: **Volume**
Fill a measuring cup with water. Pour the water into a different shaped container. **Which container holds more water?** Explain that the *volume*—the space an object takes up—does not change when the shape of the container changes.

Pages 286–287: **Density and buoyancy**
Compare the mass and volume of a loaf of bread and a brick. A loaf of bread may be larger, but a brick weighs more than a loaf of bread. The brick has more density. **You can learn about density by finding out whether or not something is buoyant—whether something floats in water.** If you place a brick in water it sinks because the brick has more density than water. The brick is not buoyant.

Page 288: **Tools that measure volume and length**
What is the difference in size and shape of the three pictures with cubic units? Less than 12 cubic units will not fill up the space of the box.

Make metric measurements of classroom objects to determine which unit of measure to use—meter or centimeter. For instance, a table or desk is best measured in meters; a pencil in centimeters.

Extend Language

Write and say different words that describe a heavy object such as a brick. (heavy, dense, weighs a lot) Invite students to list words that describe a light object (light, not dense). Then, show students a variety of objects. Help them use comparative words such as *heavier, denser, lighter, less dense.*

Every Student Learns

↻ Cause and Effect

Water and ice are made up of the same kind of matter: water. When the temperature falls to 0°C (32°F) or below, water freezes and becomes ice. The drop in temperature is the *cause*. Fill in the graphic organizer below with the *effect*.

Water to Ice

Cause		Effect
The temperature falls to the freezing point at 0°	→	

What happens when wood burns? The fire burns the wood. The wood changes to gases and ashes. Fill in the graphic organizer below to show the cause and effect.

Wood to Ashes

Cause		Effect
	→	

Lesson 1: What are physical changes in matter?

Vocabulary

*physical change	*states of matter

Activate Prior Knowledge/Build Background

Crumple a sheet of paper. Then sharpen a pencil. **How did I change the paper (pencil)?** Explain that you made a physical change to both the paper and pencil. Matter goes through a *physical change* when it changes the way it looks. **Did I change the matter of the paper and pencil?** A physical change does not cause a new kind of matter to form. **What other physical changes can you think of?**

Access Content

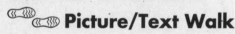 **Picture/Text Walk**

Pages 302–303: **Carved mountain, fruit**
Point to the photo of the carved face in the mountain. Emphasize that no matter what the mountain looks like, it is still made of the same rock. Only the shape has changed. Point to the fruit. Explain that even if you divide up a fruit, each portion is still made of the same kind of matter. **Is the cut-up orange made of the same matter as the whole orange? What kind of changes did the mountain and the fruit go through?** Matter goes through a physical change when it only changes the way it looks.

Page 304: **Clothes, cutting paper**
If you fold clothes, what kind of change are you making? If you cut paper, what kind of change are you making?

Page 305: **States of water**
What kind of matter do you see in each glass flask? What makes ice melt? What does ice become when it melts? What happens when you heat up water? Point out that the change from solid to liquid to gas is a physical change. The matter in each glass flask is still water, no matter what state the water is in.

Picture It! Cause and Effect

Explain that a *cause* makes something happen. An *effect* is what happens. For example, I forgot to water my plant. The plant died. The first event (forgetting to water the plant) is the cause. The second event is the effect. Guide students as they fill in the cause and effect graphic organizers.

Every Student Learns

Lesson 2: What are some ways to combine matter?

Vocabulary

*mixture	*solution	dissolve

Activate Prior Knowledge/Build Background

Bring in a simple mixture such as salt and rocks. Explain that a *mixture* is made of different kinds of matter. **What is this mixture made of?** Then mix salt in a glass container with water. Stir until the salt dissolves. **Is this a mixture?** Explain that the salt water is a *solution*. **A solution is a kind of mixture in which one kind of matter dissolves in the other. The salt *dissolves* in the water.**

Access Content

 Picture/Text Walk

Page 306: **Combining matter**
Is the salad a mixture? Why? What about the coins? Is this a mixture? Emphasize that a *mixture* is made up of two or more different kinds of matter that are placed together. The different kinds of matter that make up the mixture can be separated from one another.

Page 307: **Marbles and sand**
How are the marbles and sand like the salad? Can you separate the sand from the marbles? Is this a mixture?

Pages 308–309: **Soda can, saltwater**
Point to the soda can. **Why does the soda can fizz?** Explain that soda is a mixture of liquid and carbon dioxide gas. **If you shake a can of soda, the gas separates from the liquid. When you open the can, the gas escapes.** Point to the saltwater mixture. **Why is saltwater a *solution?*** (The salt dissolves in the water.) **Why is saltwater a mixture?** Explain that the water and the salt can be separated from one another. When the water boils away, only the salt remains.

Extend Language

Write and say the word *solution*. Explain this word has many meanings, including "answer." Have students work in groups to look up the definition for *solution* in a dictionary. Have each group write the different meanings of *solution* with an example sentence for each meaning.

Lesson 3: What are chemical changes in matter?

Vocabulary

*chemical change

Activate Prior Knowledge/Build Background

Review the lesson on physical changes. **What are some physical changes? When a physical change happens, did the kind of matter change?** Explain that there is another kind of change. **When a chemical change happens, the kind of matter changes. For example, when you light a fire, what happens to the wood? Is the wood the same before and after the fire?** Show magazine photographs of materials formed by chemical changes, such as cooked food or steel. **These things began as a mixture of materials. Heat made the matter in these mixtures change into a different kind of matter.**

Access Content

👣👣 Picture/Text Walk

Page 310: **Fried egg, baked bread**
Point to the egg. **Does this egg look the same as before it was cooked?** Point to the bread. **Does this bread look the same as before it was cooked?** Encourage students to describe changes in look, smell, or taste. **When a *chemical change* occurs, one kind of matter changes into another kind of matter.**

Page 311: **Rusted chain, campfire**
Point to the chain. **Have you ever left your bicycle in the rain? Did the rain change the metal on your bike? How?** Explain that iron and water combine with oxygen from the air to change the iron to rust. Point to the campfire. **How is the wood different before and after a fire? What is left after the wood burns?**

Pages 312–313: **Using chemical changes**
What do we use to make cars move? Explain that cars burn gasoline. The gasoline changes to energy to make the cars go. This is a chemical change. Point to the batteries. **When you use batteries, the chemicals in the batteries mix and make a small amount of electricity. This is a chemical change.** Remind students that whenever one kind of matter changes into another kind of matter, a chemical change has taken place. **Can you think of any other chemical changes?** (eating food, any kind of electricity)

© Pearson Education, Inc. 3

Every Student Learns

⊙Summarize

Read the article below. Then write a summary.

Simple machines do not lessen the amount of work you have to do. Simple machines help make work easier. Wedges split, cut, or fasten things. Screws can be used to raise and lower things. Pulleys help move objects.

Detail	Detail	Detail
Wedges split, cut, or fasten things.	Screws can be used to raise and lower things.	Pulleys help move objects.

Summary

Now write three details and a summary of the science article below.

Many forces cause a bicycle to change its motion. Your legs push on the pedals. You push on the handlebar to turn. Going downhill, you may pick up too much speed. You pull on the handbrakes to slow down.

Detail	Detail	Detail

Summary

Lesson 1: What happens when things change position?

Vocabulary

*position	*relative position	constant speed
*motion	*speed	variable speed

Activate Prior Knowledge/Build Background

Invite students to walk from your classroom to another school location, such as the library. Explain that when something changes its location, it changes its position. As students return to the classroom, ask them to remember the route. Working in small groups, have students draw a map of the return route. Ask each group to present their map to the class using words like *forward, behind, left,* and *right.*

Access Content

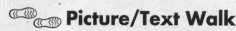 Picture/Text Walk

Page 329: **Cars on a racetrack**
Tell students to imagine that the photograph only shows Car 64. **How would you describe the car's position?** Then have students describe the position of Car 64 compared with the other cars. **Relative position is the position of one object compared with the position of other objects.**

Page 331: **Bumper cars**
Can you change the position of a bumper car? Explain that bumper cars are usually in motion. They continue to change their position. **Bumper cars also change their speed.** Speed is how fast an object changes its position. Discuss how some objects move at variable speeds, while others move at constant speeds.

Picture It! Summarize

Guide students to identify the details and summary in each article.

Lesson 2: How does force affect motion

Vocabulary

| *force | mass | *magnetism |
| *friction | *gravity | |

Activate Prior Knowledge/Build Background

Invite students to stand up and push their chairs underneath their desks. Then have them pull the chairs back out. **What caused the chairs to move?** Explain that a force is a push or a pull. A force can change an object's position or the direction of its motion.

Access Content

Picture/Text Walk

Pages 332–333: **Shopping carts**
Point to the picture of the girl pushing the lone cart. **What force is causing the cart to move?** Explain that how an object moves also depends on how much mass the object has. Direct students to look at the picture on page 333. **More carts have more mass.** Explain that the girl would have to use more force to cause multiple carts to move.

Pages 334: **Tug of war**
Which team will win? If the force of one team is greater than the other, the rope will move in that team's direction. Point out that if forces are equal, the rope will not move in either direction.

Page 335: **Bicycles**
Ask students to identify the forces that cause a bike to move. **Is it easier to ride a bike on a dirt path or on a paved path? Why?** Explain that gravel produces the greater opposing force. This opposing force is called friction. Friction is a contact force that opposes the motion of an object. Clarify that friction can cause moving objects to slow down or stop.

Page 336: **Skydivers**
Can you see the force that pulls the skydivers toward the ground? Tell students that some forces cannot be seen. Furthermore, some forces do not need to make contact with an object. Gravity is one of these noncontact forces.

© Pearson Education, Inc. 3

Lesson 3: How do simple machines work?

Vocabulary

*work	screw	axle
inclined plane	lever	pulley
wedge	wheel	

Activate Prior Knowledge/Build Background

Prompt students to identify machines in the classroom. List these machines. **How do machines help us?** Explain that machines help people do work.

Access Content

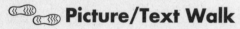 Picture/Text Walk

Page 338: **Soccer ball and snowball**
Invite volunteers to share some of the work they do in a day. Point to the picture of the soccer ball being kicked. **Is this work?** Explain that work happens when you use a force to move an object. Then point to the picture of children trying to move the snowball. **The snowball is not moving. Is this work? Why or why not?**

Pages 340–343: **Simple machines**
Simple machines make work easier. Point to the simple machines pictured on each page. Name each machine; explain how it helps us do work. Review the list of classroom machines you made earlier. Identify the simple machines listed there. You could also help students to identify the simple machines that make up the more complex machinery listed.

Extend Language

Write and say *incline* and *decline*. **How are these words different?** Invite a volunteer to circle the prefixes *in-* and *de-*. Explain that the prefixes differentiate the meanings of the two words. *Incline* means "to slope up." *Decline* means "to slope down."

Every Student Learns

Main Idea and Supporting Details

Complete the chart.

We change sources of energy into electricity. We change the power of moving water into electricity. We turn the heat of burning coal into electricity. We even turn sunlight into electricity. We depend on electricity for most of our everyday needs.

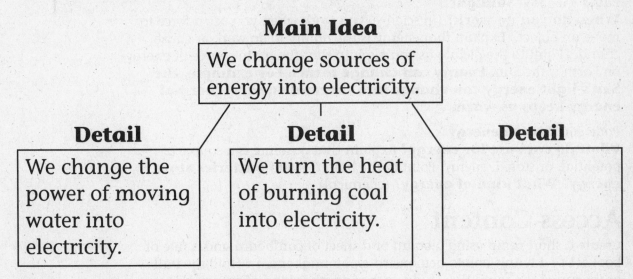

Main Idea

We change sources of energy into electricity.

Detail

We change the power of moving water into electricity.

Detail

We turn the heat of burning coal into electricity.

Detail

Now complete the chart below.

Light is a form of energy. We can see some of the ways that light changes. Light can bounce off objects. Refraction causes light to bend. Light can be absorbed by an object.

Main Idea

Detail

Detail

Detail

© Pearson Education, Inc. 3

Lesson 1: What is energy?

Vocabulary

energy	*potential energy	*kinetic energy
motion	position	

Activate Prior Knowledge/Build Background

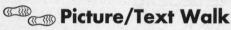 **Picture/Text Walk**

Pages 358–359: **Sunlight**
When do you do work? (In science, you work when you use a force to move an object.) Explain that energy is the ability to do work or cause change. Point to the picture as you explain that the main source of energy on Earth is the Sun. **Energy can change forms. For example, the Sun's light energy can change into thermal energy. Thermal energy keeps us warm.**

Page 360: **Stored energy**
What do cars use for energy? Explain that gasoline is a source of potential, or stored, energy. Point to the batteries. **Do batteries store energy? What kind of energy?** (chemical)

Access Content

Create a short ramp using a board or a sheet of cardboard and a pile of books. Use a tennis ball to demonstrate potential energy. Hold the ball at the top of the ramp. Tell students that another kind of energy has to do with height. **The tennis ball has potential energy at the top of the ramp. This potential energy changes to kinetic energy when the ball rolls down the ramp.** Explain that kinetic energy is the energy of motion. Let the ball roll down the ramp. Then, pass the ball to a volunteer. Ask the student to use the ball as another volunteer explains how potential energy changes into kinetic energy.

Picture It! Main Idea and Supporting Details

Encourage students to read each science article. Then guide students in completing each graphic organizer.
Answers: Main idea: Light is a form of energy. Details: Light can bounce. Refraction causes light to bend. Light can be absorbed.

© Pearson Education, Inc. 3

Every Student Learns

Lesson 2: How does energy change form?

Vocabulary

ripple	crest	trough

Activate Prior Knowledge/Build Background

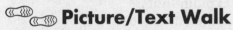 **Picture/Text Walk**

Page 363: **Forms of energy**
Point to the vegetables in the chart. **What kind of energy is this?**
Repeat the experience with each picture, asking students to look at each
picture and name the kind of energy shown. Ask them to provide other
examples of each kind of energy.

Page 364: **Ways that energy travels**
Point to the ocean waves. **Do waves carry energy? What kind of
energy?** (kinetic) Point to the waves in the bucket. **Where is this
energy coming from?** Explain that energy from the falling drop moves
in waves across the water.

Access Content

 **Picture/Text Walk**

Page 365: **Parts of a wave**
Show students the wave pattern on page 365. Tell students that we can
measure the amount of energy a wave carries. Illustrate how a wave's
width is measured. **Wide waves have more energy than waves
that are narrow.** Then, illustrate how the length of an energy wave is
measured. **Waves that are short have lots of energy. Longer waves
have less energy.** Use a rope to model the wave pattern shown. Invite
volunteers to experiment with different speeds and amounts of energy
to change the wave's length and width. You may wish to mark the rope
with masking tape to illustrate that the rope does not move forward; it
moves up and down as energy travels from one end of the rope to the
other. **Where does the rope's energy come from?** (from the students'
movements)

Lesson 3: What is heat energy?

Vocabulary

*thermal energy	water	expand
friction	vapor	
evaporate	boil	

Activate Prior Knowledge/Build Background

Do you feel warmer or cooler after you exercise? Explain that body temperature rises because some kinetic energy is changed into heat energy.

Access Content

〰️ **Picture/Text Walk**

Page 366: **Cup and spoon**
Ask students if they have ever placed a metal spoon into a cup or bowl of a hot liquid. **What happened to the spoon?** Explain that thermal energy from the hot liquid travels through the spoon. This is what causes the spoon to feel warm to the touch. The flow of energy stops when the temperature of the liquid and the spoon are the same.

Page 367: **Matches**
Encourage students to rub their hands together. Invite volunteers to describe what is happening, what they feel. **Rubbing your hands together causes friction. Friction gives off heat.** Every time energy moves, there is heat.

Page 369: **Boiling water**
What does boiling water look like? Explain to students that heat can make liquid water change in another way. At a temperature of 100°C, heat makes water boil. Point to the bottom of the flask. **Heat makes the water expand, or get bigger. The water becomes a gas. Gas bubbles float to the top of the water. The bubbles break open and release hot water droplets.**

Extend Language

Explain that *thermal* comes from the Greek word meaning heat. Have students use a dictionary to find the meanings for the related words, such as *thermometer* and *thermostat*. Encourage students to use the words in sentences.

© Pearson Education, Inc. 3

Lesson 4: What is light energy?

Vocabulary

shadow	*refract	*absorb
*reflect	images	separate

Activate Prior Knowledge/Build Background

Use a flashlight to demonstrate the ways in which light behaves. **Does light travel in a straight line?** (yes) **Will it bend around a corner?** (no) **What happens when I shine the light on a mirror?**

Access Content

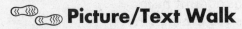 **Picture/Text Walk**

Page 371: **Shadows**
Did the light from our flashlight bend around corners? Explain that shadows are created because light does not bend or turn. It travels in a straight line until an object stops it. Point to the picture. **Shadows are areas behind objects that are not getting direct light.** The length of the shadow depends on the angle of the light.

Page 372: **How light changes**
Point out how the image in the lake is the same as the trees being reflected. However, the reflected image is upside down. Describe how light bounces off the lake and back to our eyes. Emphasize that all objects reflect light. But smooth, flat surfaces reflect light better than other surfaces. Explain how water can refract, or bend, light, causing it to change direction. It can make objects look different.

Page 373: **Straw in a glass of water**
What's wrong with this straw? Tell students that in reality, the straw is made of one complete piece. The straw looks broken because light passing through the air slows down when it enters the water. The water caused the light to refract and make the straw look bent.

Extend Language

Point out that you can add the suffix *-ion* to the verbs *reflect* and *refract* to form the nouns *reflection* and *refraction*. Encourage students to use these words in sentences.

© Pearson Education, Inc. 3

Lesson 5: What is electrical energy?

Vocabulary

*electric charge	*electric current	controlled
positive	uncontrolled	*electric circuit
negative		

Activate Prior Knowledge/Build Background

Rub a balloon on a volunteer's hair. Ask students to predict what will happen when the balloon touches a piece of paper. (the paper sticks to the balloon) Invite another volunteer to rub two balloons against his or her hair. **What happens when we put the balloons together? (**the balloons push away from each other) Explain that these examples show the powers of electrical energy. **An electric charge is a tiny amount of energy and all matter has electric charges.**

Access Content

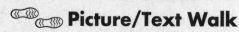 **Picture/Text Walk**

Page 376: **Electric circuit**
Electric current is the movement of electric charges or electrical energy from one place to another. Explain that in order for an electric current to be useful, it must move in a planned way through wires or other materials. **An electric circuit is the path that a controlled electric current flows through.** Have students follow the path of electricity with their fingers as you explain each numbered diagram label. Point out that when the switch is flipped up to the "off" position, the flow of energy in the circuit stops.

Page 377: **Electricity changes forms**
Review each form of energy on the chart. Then ask students to identify other objects that might be used to illustrate each form of energy. For example, electricity is changed into light energy when a string of holiday lights or a spotlight are used.

Compare and Contrast

Look at the pictures. Then study the graphic organizer to see how vocal cords and wind instruments make sound.

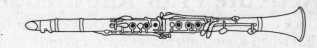

How Vocal Cords and Wind Instruments Make Sound

Vocal Cords
1. vocal cords vibrate

Both
1. vibration causes sound

Wind Instruments
1. air moves through clarinet.

Compare and Contrast

Sound travels more slowly through gases than through solids. Describe the differences between gases and solids in the diagram below. In the part labeled *Both* describe what is the same.

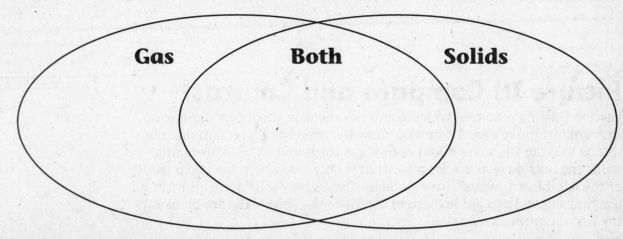

Gas   **Both**   **Solids**

Lesson 1: What causes sounds?

Vocabulary

*vibrations	*pitch	volume

Activate Prior Knowledge/Build Background

Pluck a stretched rubber band. **What do you see and hear?** Explain that when something moves back and forth it causes *vibrations*. Sound only happens when something vibrates.

Access Content

Pages 391–392: **How to describe sound**
Say something in a voice higher than usual. Then say something in a voice lower than usual. How were the sounds the same or different? *Pitch* describes how high or low a sound is.

Picture/Text Walk

Page 393: **Percussion and string instruments**
Ask students to compare what they do to make sounds with their vocal cords to what they would do to make sounds with the harp or blocks. Explain that you can create vibrations in different ways—like humming, or plucking a string, or hitting a block. But only vibrations make sound happen.

Pages 394–395: **The human voice and wind instruments**
Read the caption for the illustration of vocal cords on page 394 and have students follow the directions. **What can you feel? What do you hear?** Sound happens only when something moves back and forth to cause *vibrations*. **When you blow into the wind instruments you see on these pages, how is it like creating sound with your vocal cords?** (The air you blow vibrates in the wind instruments; your vocal cords vibrate in your throat.)

Picture It! Compare and Contrast

Discuss the first diagram, which compares the way vocal cords and wind instruments make sound. Point out how the overlapping section describes things that are the same about both vocal cords and wind instruments, while the outside sections describe what is only true about the vocal cords or the wind instruments. Have students discuss how sound travels through gas and solids. Then guide them to complete the Venn diagram by using the first diagram as a model.

Every Student Learns

Lesson 2: How does sound travel?

Vocabulary

*compression wave

Activate Prior Knowledge/Build Background

Tie a piece of rope approximately 10 feet long to an object that is about 3 feet above the ground. Hold the end of the rope and dangle it. Then move the rope faster and faster until it blurs and makes a sound like wind. **What do you see and hear?**

Access Content

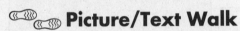 **Picture/Text Walk**

Pages 396–397: **Compression waves from sound**
Point to the photograph and illustration on page 398. **How does the sound travel from the jackhammer?** Explain that vibrations create sound waves that travel through matter. Particles that make up matter in the path of the sound wave squeeze together and spread apart. This is a called a *compression wave*. Point out how a compression wave carries energy like the coils in a spring.

Pages 398–399: **Sound and matter**
Have students work in pairs. One student knocks on a tabletop. The student knocks again, but this time the partner puts an ear to the table and listens. **How is the sound different when you hear it in the air and on the tabletop?** Particles in solids are closer together than particles in gases or particles in liquids. The closer the particles are, the more quickly the energy of a sound wave can move through matter.

Page 400: **The ear**
Ask students to look at the picture and point to the part of the ear on the outside of the body. Invite them to follow the path that sound makes as it travels to the eardrum and little bones to the inner ear. Explain that the brain receives a message that sound has happened from nerves attached to the inner ear.

Extend Language

Explain that some expressions such as "keep your ear to the ground" are confusing because even if you know what each word means, the phrase means something completely different. Ask if anyone knows the meaning of this expression. (to listen carefully, hoping to get early warning about something). Together, make up sentences with this idiom and write them on the board. Invite students to copy the sentences and draw humorous illustrations for each one.

↻ Sequence

The length and direction of shadows change during the day. In the morning and evening, shadows are very long. In the middle of the day, shadows are short. The shadow is always in the opposite direction of the Sun. If the Sun rises in the east, a morning shadow will stretch to the west.

| 7:00 A.M. | 12:00 P.M. | 5:00 P.M. |

Look at the pictures. Then draw the object and the shadow as it would look at 5:00 P.M.

Make a diagram that shows how the shadow of a flagpole will change during the day.

| 7:00 A.M. | 12:00 P.M. | 5:00 P.M. |

Lesson 1: What are some patterns that repeat every day?

Vocabulary

*star   *rotation
*axis   shadow

Activate Prior Knowledge/Build Background

Brainstorm with students a list of patterns that repeat every day. Students may point out, for example, that day always changes to night and back again. Shadows start out long, become shorter, and become long again on a sunny day. If students have trouble identifying patterns, give them hints such as: **How does the Sun seem to move each day?**

Access Content

 **Picture/Text Walk**

Page 424: **Earth spinning on its axis**
Use the illustration to discuss how Earth spinning on its axis causes day and night. If possible, illustrate this pattern of night and day with a ball and a flashlight. Ask: **What makes it appear that the Sun rises and sets in the sky?**

Page 425: **Sun's movement**
During what times of day is the Sun low in the sky? When is the Sun high in the sky? Explain to students that Earth's rotation takes 24 hours and that is why a complete day on Earth is 24 hours long.

Page 426: **Shadows**
Discuss with students how the shadow will stretch to the west when the Sun is in the east. Ask: **Why don't you see shadows on a cloudy day?**

Page 427: **Sun rising**
Use the sequence of pictures to discuss how shadows change based on the apparent location of the Sun.

Picture It! Sequence

Explain to students that many events occur in patterns. This often helps us to determine the sequence of events. Guide students as they draw the third picture in the box. Discuss how at 5 P.M. the shadow stretches in the opposite direction than it stretched in the morning (draw shadow stretching behind goal). Guide students to draw the sequence of a flag pole's shadow during the day.

© Pearson Education, Inc. 3

Every Student Learns

Lesson 2: What patterns repeat every year?

Vocabulary

*revolution	season

Activate Prior Knowledge/Build Background

Ask students to name the four seasons. Encourage a discussion of typical weather for each season and ask students to describe the clothing they might wear during each season. As students brainstorm suggestions, write their ideas on the board. Then ask: **How do you know what the weather will be like?** Guide students to understand that the seasons occur in a predictable pattern and that there are particular weather features of each season that are also predictable.

Access Content

 **Picture/Text Walk**

Pages 428–429: **Earth's position during the year**
Discuss with students how direct sunlight causes warmer temperatures on Earth. Use the diagram and invite students to point to each of Earth's positions. At each position ask: **What half of Earth is tilted towards the Sun? What is the weather like in the northern hemisphere?**

Page 429: **Direct rays**
Use the model to illustrate to students how the Sun's direct rays are more focused on one area, which means they heat Earth more than rays that strike at an angle. You might also use a ball and a flashlight to help students see how the angled rays spread out over a greater area.

Pages 430–431: **The Sun's position in the sky**
Discuss with students how Earth's tilted axis makes it seem that the Sun is in different places in the sky during different seasons. **When the Sun is lower in the sky, are the temperatures higher? Are there more hours of daylight when the Sun is higher in the sky or lower in the sky?**

Extend Language

Ask students to draw a diagram of Earth's positions around the Sun with a dotted line showing the *axis* and arrows to indicate Earth's *revolution*. Have students label each of their diagrams and keep them in their science folders to refer to during the chapter.

© Pearson Education, Inc. 3

Lesson 3: Why does the Moon's shape change?

Vocabulary

*phase	eclipse

Activate Prior Knowledge/Build Background

Encourage a discussion of all the different ways the Moon looks. Show students pictures of the Moon during its different phases. **How do you know that these are all pictures of the Moon?** Explain to students that the Moon's shape changes in a pattern.

Access Content

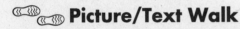 Picture/Text Walk

Page 432: **The Moon revolving around Earth**
How long does it take for the Moon to rotate one time? How long does it take for the Moon to revolve around Earth? Explain to students that because of these movements, the same side of the Moon always faces Earth.

Pages 433–434: **Earth and the Moon**
How big is the Moon compared to Earth? Discuss with students how we can see the Moon at night even though it does not make its own light.

Page 434: **Lunar eclipse**
What makes a shadow on the Moon during a lunar eclipse? Where is Earth during a lunar eclipse?

Page 435: **Phases of the Moon**
What phase of the Moon happens about a week after the New Moon? (first quarter) **Which phases of the Moon looks like a lighted circle?** (full Moon) **Why can't the Moon be seen during the New Moon?** Explain to students that the phases of the Moon always follow the same pattern.

Lesson 4: Star patterns

Vocabulary

*telescope	*constellation	binoculars

Activate Prior Knowledge/Build Background

Show or draw some pictures of the Big Dipper and Little Dipper constellations with the stars connected with lines. Ask if anyone has heard of the Big Dipper or the Little Dipper. Ask students who have heard of the constellations to explain what they know about each constellation. Tell students that the Big Dipper and Little Dipper are two patterns of stars that can be seen in the night sky.

Access Content

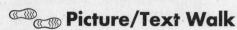 **Picture/Text Walk**

Page 436: **Keck telescope**
How does a telescope help us study the night sky? How is this huge Keck telescope like a smaller telescope that you might use?
(They both use tubes, mirrors, and lenses to make larger and clearer views of objects in the sky.)

Page 437: **Person with binoculars**
Discuss with students the purpose of binoculars and how they are similar to and different from telescopes. Students should understand that telescopes are generally more powerful than binoculars.

Page 439: **Big Dipper and Little Dipper**
How do the positions of the Big Dipper and Little Dipper change between summer and winter? Do the stars actually move in the sky, or do they appear to move in the sky?

Page 439: **Time lapse photograph**
Explain that during time lapse photography, photos are taken at regular intervals so that changes can easily be seen. Ask students to describe the star tracks and say why they think the tracks appear as curved lines.

Extend Language

Point out that many verbs that end with a short vowel and a single consonant, such as *dip*, can be turned into nouns by doubling the last letter and adding -er. Work together to make a poster of words that follow this pattern (stop, rob, win, dig, swim, rap, rub, etc.) and invite students to illustrate it.

Every Student Learns

↻ Compare and Contrast

Study the graphic organizer to see how planets and asteroids are alike and are different.

Planet
1. large body of matter that revolves around the Sun
2. rotates in place while it orbits Sun

Both
1. found in solar system
2. orbits around Sun
3. held in orbit by gravity

Asteroid
1. chunk of rock usually found between Mars and Jupiter
2. orbits Sun but does not rotate

Compare and Contrast Inner and Outer Planets

Complete the graphic organizer to show how the inner planets and outer planets are alike and different.

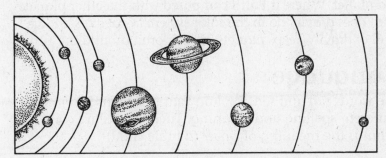

Inner Planets   **Both**   **Outer Planets**

Lesson 1: What are the parts of the solar system?

Vocabulary

*planet	*orbit
*solar system	*asteroids

Activate Prior Knowledge/Build Background

Invite students to describe what they see in the night sky. **How does what you see in the sky at night compare with what you see in the sky during the day?** Explain that the Sun is a star, but it is much closer to Earth than other stars.

Access Content

Pages 454–455: **The Sun**
Why is the Sun important to Earth? Explain that the Sun is a ball of hot, glowing gases. The temperature of the Sun produces energy that lights and warms Earth.

Picture/Text Walk

Pages 456–457: **The solar system**
With students, point to and name the planets from the most outer to the most inner planet. All the planets and the Sun make up the *solar system*. **Where is the Sun?** Explain that the nine planets revolve around the Sun in oval paths called *orbits*. Explain that an *asteroid* is a chunk of rock that orbits the Sun; it is not a planet. Where is Earth compared with the other planets and the Sun? What does gravity do in the solar system? Gravity is a force that pulls. The pull of gravity keeps planets in their orbit around the Sun.

Extend Language

Write and say the words *sun* and *son*. Explain that some words sound alike but have different spelling and meaning. These words are called homophones. What is the meaning of *s-o-n?* (a male child)

Picture It! Compare and Contrast

Discuss the first diagram, which compares how planets and asteroids are alike and different. Encourage students to discuss characteristics of the inner and outer planets. Then guide them to complete the Venn diagram (Inner Planets: closest to Sun, rocky; Outer Planets: farther from Sun, mostly made of gas; Alike: all part of solar system).

© Pearson Education, Inc. 3

Lesson 2: What are the planets?

Vocabulary

revolution	rotation

Activate Prior Knowledge/Build Background

What do you think is the most special thing about our planet?
Explain that every planet has special features. From space, you can see
the blue oceans of Earth. Because of that, Earth is often called the "blue
planet."

Access Content

Demonstrate Earth's movement during a 1-day rotation and a 1-year
revolution. Have a volunteer act as the Sun and stand in an open area.
Have another volunteer act as Earth and walk in one full circle around
the Sun. When Earth orbits the Sun, one full revolution takes 365 days
and 6 hours. That is the length of 1 year. Have Earth turn around in
place. While Earth spins in place, one full rotation takes 24 hours. That is
the length of 1 day. Have Earth make half of a rotation so his or her back
faces the Sun. **What part of Earth has daylight? Nighttime?** During
a rotation, the surface of Earth facing the Sun has daylight. The surface
of Earth that does not face the Sun has nighttime. Point out that Earth
rotates on a tilt.

Picture/Text Walk

Pages 460–461: **Life on Earth**
How do the blue parts of Earth support life? Explain that water
and the right mix of gases in the atmosphere support living things. **What
else about Earth supports living things?** (Mild temperatures plus the
right amount of light to help living things grow.)

Pages 462–465: **The outer planets**
What are the names of the outer planets? (Jupiter, Saturn, Uranus,
Neptune, and Pluto.) These outer planets are not rocky like the inner
planets of Mercury, Venus, Earth, and Mars. The outer planets are called gas
giants because, except for Pluto, they are huge and made mostly of gas

Pages 463–464 **Rings and other features**
Explain that every planet has its own special features. **What is a special
feature of Saturn and Uranus?** Explain that some planets have rings,
many moons, belts of asteroids that orbit around them, or other distinct
features such as Jupiter's Great Red Spot.

⊙ Sequence

Complete the sentence to describe the sequence.

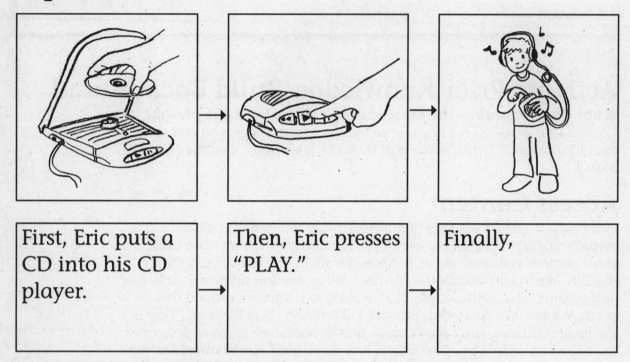

First, Eric puts a CD into his CD player.

Then, Eric presses "PLAY."

Finally,

Fill in the graphic organizer to describe the sequence.

First,

Then,

Finally,

© Pearson Education, Inc. 3

Lesson 1: How does technology affect our lives?

Vocabulary

*tool	*invention
*technology	system

Activate Prior Knowledge/Build Background

Hold up a ruler. **Is this a tool?** Hold up a pair of scissors. **Is this a tool? Why do we use tools?** (tools make work easier) **What are some other tools we use in school?**

Access Content

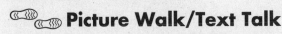 **Picture Walk/Text Talk**

Pages 478–479: **Roman arches**
Technology is the use of knowledge to design new tools and new ways of doing things. Explain that something made for the first time is an invention. **These arches were an invention. They brought water from the mountain springs to cities. Would you like to invent a tool? What would it do?**

Page 480: **Home technology**
Explain that different parts of a building may work together as systems. **You use a plumbing system when you flush the toilet. The electrical system heats this water.** Use the chart and pictures on page 480 to point out other home systems.

Pages 482–483: **Future technology**
Use the pictures to point out how technology has advanced over time. Then, share some ideas about future technology. Suggest that some people believe computers will run the entire home, and a computer chip in a food package will tell the oven how to cook it. Perhaps refrigerators will be connected to the Internet. **Do you think these ideas will happen? Why or why not?**

Picture It! Sequence

Explain that a sequence is a series of actions that happen in a certain order. Point out that words such as *first*, *then*, and *finally* signal a sequence. Help students identify the sequence in each set of pictures.

© Pearson Education, Inc. 3

Lesson 2: What are some new technologies?

Vocabulary

global positioning system (GPS)   optical fibers *computer   microwave

Activate Prior Knowledge/Build Background

Hold up a map with a legend. **This is a map. What do we use it for?**
Point out the directions north, south, east, and west. **Today, we have easier ways to find out where we are and where we need to go.**

Access Content

⤇ Picture Walk/Text Talk

Page 484: **Satellite and maps**
Now, we use Global Positioning Systems (GPS) to help us find our way. Explain how a GPS receives signals from a satellite. **The GPS system is used by navigators to find out where they are and to plot a route. A GPS can also make maps and pictures. Some cars have GPS.**

Page 485: **Optical fibers**
A computer stores, processes, and sends electronic information very quickly. Do you use a computer at home? What do you do on it? Explain how optical fibers make computers better because they take up less space than wires.

Page 488: **Microwave oven**
Have you ever used a microwave? What can microwaves do?
Tell students the story of Percy Spencer and how he invented microwaves. Stress how some technologies become useful in unplanned ways.

Extend Language

Write *global positioning system*. Circle the first letter in each word. **We can also call a global positioning system a GPS system. GPS is an abbreviation. Abbreviations are shorter forms of longer words or terms.** Write *liquid crystal display*. **What is the abbreviation of this word?** (LCD) Challenge students to also figure out these abbreviations: *personal computer* (PC), *compact disc* (CD), *digital video disc* (DVD). Encourage students to brainstorm other abbreviations they may know.

© Pearson Education, Inc. 3

Lesson 3: How does technology help us get energy?

Vocabulary

energy	windmill	renewable
water mill	pollute	solar panel

Activate Prior Knowledge/Build Background

Remind students that technology is the use of knowledge to design new tools and new ways of doing things. **Technology has changed the way we get energy.** Explain that we continue to use technology to find new and cleaner energy resources.

Access Content

Picture Walk/Text Talk

Pages 490–491: **Water wheel and windmill**
Have you ever seen a water wheel or a windmill? Explain that water wheels and windmills were used to do work. They were powered by water and the wind. Both wind and water are renewable resources that do not pollute the environment. Tell students that both are still used, though not as widely.

Pages 492–493: **Generators and the Hoover Dam**
Point out the Hoover Dam on page 493. Describe how dams are built on rivers; the river backs up behind the dam to form a lake. The lake's water stores energy. **The energy in this dam is used to make electricity. This is called hydroelectric power.** Point to the generators on page 492. Discuss the role of water wheel technology in making hydroelectric power.

Pages 494–495: **Solar panels**
Explain how solar panels are attached to the roof of a building. The panels collect sunlight. **The panels change sunlight into solar energy. Solar energy can be used for electricity or it can be used to heat water.** Like wind and water, the Sun's energy is a renewable resource.